Welcome to Reflection in Practise.

Created by educators, for educators.

2018 NQS Element 1.3.2: Critical reflection: Critical reflection on children's learning and development, both as individuals and in groups, drives program planning and implementation.

In education and care services, critical reflection means 'Closely examining all aspects of events and experiences from different perspectives' (Approved Learning Frameworks – EYLF p.13, FSAC p.12).

https://www.acecqa.gov.au/sites/default/files/2019-08/What%20is%20Critical%20Reflection.pdf

Critical reflection is a crucial part of our role as educators, but often we find it the hardest thing to do. Why? Because, we see it as a bad thing "critical = criticise". In truth, critical reflection is the pulling apart of an experience – examining its parts and reconstructing it in a way that brings meaning to it. It is very easy to fall into the trap of simply observing rather than reflecting. For critical reflection to be effective it needs to be regular, consistent, cyclic, purposeful, and honest. We all make mistakes – we are human after all – critical reflection can help us identify what went wrong and ways to improve our practice. Of course, we all have great moments too – these are often harder for us to recognise and we can rely too heavily on others to tell us when we are doing a great job – Critical Reflection can help us to identify these moments, accept and celebrate them, and use them to improve our practice (see what I did there?)

Why did I create this journal? I have been involved in childcare, in various capacities, for over 20 years, 15 of those in OSHC, working as both an educator and a manager. In that time, my experience has been that there are very few tools out there specifically for OSHC educators, and many that are available are repetitive and boring, thinly veiled adaptations of LDC templates, or geared towards managers and decision makers rather than every-day out-on-the-floor educators. The result of this is repetitive recording, simple observation, or nothing at all. The purpose of this journal is to take us out of the paperwork drudgery into a fun, insightful and (hopefully) useful form of reflection that will improve our practice and help us grow as educators, resulting in better outcomes for the children in our care.

Happy and engaged educators = Happy and engaged children.

So, join us on a reflective journey. This book has been designed in 2 parts, a weekly section with plenty of space for notes, questions, and activities to reflect on our practice, and a monthly section with information, recipes, activity ideas, and reflective questions. Please use both parts together. If you like what you find here, please share the news with other educators and managers. Any feedback can be emailed to hbrown19561@gmail.com.

Happy reflecting!

*Note for managers and educational leaders. While this journal has been specifically created for educators, there are many useful reflective sections suitable for managers and ed. leaders. Many of the questions may be useful for group reflective discussions as well.

*note for agency staff or educators who work in multiple services, some parts of this book may not seem relevant to you. For those bits, use your favourite service, one you visit regularly, or an "in an ideal world" service for reference.

Please contact the publishers directly at the above email for a discount on bulk purchases (10 books or more).

Copyright © Reading Stones Publishing 2020

ISBN: 978-0-6485285-6-2

All rights reserved. No part of this book may be reproduced or transmitted in any form or by any means, electronic, or mechanical, including photocopying, recording or by any information storage and retrieval system without the permission in writing by the copyright owner.

Stock images from:	Shutterstock.<Shutterstock.com>
	Storyblocks <storyblocks.com>

Quotes and associated artworks supplied by:	Helen Brown - The Helen Brown Collection
	Dawn Kelly
	Jennifer Maybury – In Your Eyes Photography

Information on the National Quality System and My Time Our Place – Framework for School Age Care in Australia from:	The Australian Children's Education and Care Quality Authority <acecqa.gov.au>

Please see reference page for other reference sites used in the creation of this book.

Published by:	Reading Stones Publishing < https://woodwendy1982.wixsite.com/readingstones >
	Helen Brown and Wendy Wood
Cover Design:	Wendy Wood

Copies available from your favourite online retailer.

For bulk orders (10 copies or more) please contact Reading Stones for a quote at:

Glenburnie Homestead
212 Glenburnie Road
ROB ROY NSW 2360
Mobile: 0422 577 663
Email: hbrown19561@gmail.com
https://woodwendy1982.wixsite.com/readingstones

Find us on Facebook: Reading Stones Proofreading and Editing Services

Instructions – weekly pages.

This book is designed to be used in a lineal fashion. Please use each week in order and start any time of year. If you miss a week, take leave etc, just continue on from the last week you completed. i.e. don't skip pages. Each week consists of 6 boxes to be completed, 3 of these repeat weekly, others every month and some less often. Each box will ask you to reflect on part of your service, complete a challenge or activity, or provide a suggestion. As you work through this booklet, you will learn about yourself, your strengths and the things that challenge you. As you know yourself better, you become empowered to be better educators and provide better outcomes for the children in your care.

Definitions:

Program: More than just the list of activities you do each day, the program refers to everything that happens within the session of care – from arrival, to transitions, mealtimes and of course, activities.

Interactions: Any time you have a conversation, or someone talks at you, or a child takes your hand – this is an interaction. For the purpose of this book, interactions fall into 3 categories, positive, negative and neutral.

Reflection: Reflection means to consider the activity or interaction from a new perspective. Sometimes the questions will be provided for you, sometimes not. A list of reflective prompts is provided on the next page to help with this process.

Intentional Teaching: Teaching does not need to be pre-planned to be intentional. We are presented with multiple moments each day that invite intentional teaching. Look for and embrace these moments.

Flow: The uninterrupted focus on an activity or process. Children will engage in flow on their own terms when they are invested in what is happening.

Beliefs: In this context we are not talking about religion, but about our core beliefs as educators. This affects our work with children. E.g. if we believe that children are capable learners, then we will give them opportunities to do things for themselves.

Pedagogy: Is the art or science of the teaching profession. It is also the principles, practice and work of a teacher. Your pedagogy influences the way you work with children

Philosophy: Your personal philosophy is your beliefs put into action: e.g. I believe… therefore I do… this ties together your beliefs and your pedagogy.

Instructions:

Weekly notes section: A section has been provided each week for note taking – this is your page to do with as you wish, however, I suggest you use it to take notes about your work, hours, services (if you work at different sites), things you want to remember, observations and challenges.

Challenges: Throughout the pages of this book are challenges designed to help you to know yourself, or to reflect on your work as an educator. Some of them are silly, some serious. Working through the challenges will help you get the most out of this book, but if you choose not to complete the challenges, I ask you to reflect on why you chose that path.

Activity Reflections: Each week there is a space to reflect on an activity – this is basically a learning story – use this space to inform your program and develop consistent use of activity extensions.

Interaction Reflections: A big part of our job is interacting with others – children, parents, co-workers, management and members of the school community. Each week you will be asked to reflect on one of these interactions. Be honest with yourself.

Program and menu suggestions: A space is provided each week to record a menu and program suggestion. This does not need to be your own suggestion, but please record who suggested it. Make sure you share this information with the decision makers at your service (this is a great way to show that children's suggestions are incorporated into the service menu and program).

Reflective prompts

Use these to prompt your reflections.

What happened? What did I see? What did I feel?

What did I hear? Was it what I expected? Why or why not?

Which children were involved? What learning is happening? How do I know?

Was I involved? Why or why not? Did the children need my assistance? How did I know?

Did I intervene or assist at the right time? Too early? Too late?

What emotions do I see? How do I know?

What could I have done differently? How does this meet the outcomes of MTOP or NQS?

Was this unusual? Why? What interactions did I observe?

How can I extend on this?

Did I make the most of this opportunity?

Did I interrupt the children? Did I need to? What effect did that have on their play?

Do I observe flow? How do I know?

What did I expect? Could I have foreseen this outcome?

Why did I feel like this? How can I improve my practise?

What factors could be affecting the way I feel?

What did I learn from this? What theories do I see at play here?

Does this affect my pedagogy? Philosophy? Beliefs?

This is the journal of _____ Started _____

Use this space to reflect on your starting point… don't use the whole space up front, we will revisit this later.

Things I'm Good At (Strengths)	Areas I need to Improve (Challenges)

My Beliefs, Pedagogy and Philosophy

Use this space to record your core beliefs about children
I believe:

Use this space to record your Pedagogy

Use this space to record your Philosophy: Use the format: I believe, therefore I...
(e.g. I believe that children are capable learners, therefore, I provide them with opportunities to develop new skills.)

Weekly Notes and Review

> "If I speak of myself in different ways, that is because I look at myself in different ways."
>
> – Michel de Montaigne,

NOTES

God has made you stronger than you feel,
More talented than you believe,
More courageous than you think,
And He will walk with you every step of the way.

Reflect on your physical environment. Dot point 3 things you like, and 3 you would like to change.

Suggest an item for the menu: Who's idea was it? (yours/another educator/child/family)

Suggest a program activity: note whose idea it was.

Don't forget to pass these suggestions on to your manager/menu planner

Week 1 reflection. Date: _____

Think about an activity you did with the children….
What was the activity?

Whose idea was it?

How involved were you?

Could you have been more/less involved? What would you change?

How can you extend on this activity? Plan to do it next week.

Choose one day this week and set a silly goal (E.g. use the word "supercallafragalistic" 10 times)
What was the goal?

Did you achieve it? _____ if no, why?

How did others react (children, educators, parents)?

How did you feel?

Did this affect your practise? How?

---

why did the chicken cross the road?
To get to the other side of course!

Consider an interaction you had with a child this week.
Was it positive/negative? Why?

Would you have done something different? Why/why not?

How did this interaction affect your relationship with them?

What did you learn? How will this be reflected in your practise?

NOTES

Suggest an item for the menu: Who's idea was it? (yours/another educator/child/family)

Suggest a program activity: note whose idea it was.

Don't forget to pass these suggestions on to your manager/menu planner.

Reflect on inclusion in your service. Dot point one thing you do well, and one to improve

Week 2 reflection. Date: _____

Pick a child with whom you have mainly negative interactions. Plan positive interactions with the child. Try to double the number each day i.e. 1 on Monday, 2 on Tuesday, 4 on Wednesday etc.
Reflect: did you achieve the goal? Why/why not?

What did you learn about the child?

Did you notice and change in the child's attitude towards you? Explain:

Did you notice any change in your attitude towards the child? Explain:

How will this affect your work with this or other children?

Think about an activity you did with the children….
What was the activity?

Whose idea was it?
How involved were you?

Could you have been more/less involved?

What would you change?

How can you extend on this activity? Plan to do it next week.

Follow-up:
Reflect on last week's environment question. How can you make one of the changes you would like to see?

"I dream of a better tomorrow, where chickens can cross the road and not be questioned about their motives." – Ralph Waldo Emerson

Consider an interaction you had with a parent this week.
Was it positive/negative? Why?

Would you have done something different? Why/why not?

How did this interaction affect your relationship with them?

What did you learn? How will this be reflected in your practise?

NOTES

Reflect on the services routines: Dot point 3 things you like and 3 that you would like to change and how.
*Choose one of these and discuss it with your manager.

Suggest an item for the menu: Who's idea was it? (yours/another educator/child/family)

Suggest a program activity: note whose idea it was.

Don't forget to pass these suggestions on to your manager/menu planner.

Sometimes you just have to jump in and start swimming.

Week 3 reflection. Date: _____

Think about an activity you did with the children....
What was the activity?

Whose idea was it?
How involved were you?

Could you have been more/less involved?
What would you change?

How can you extend on this activity? Plan to do it next week.

Consider an interaction you had with a co-worker this week.
Was it positive/negative? Why?

Would you have done something different? Why/why not?

How did this interaction affect your relationship with them?

What did you learn? How will this be reflected in your practise?

Reflect on the program at your service.
What input do you have?

What input do the children have?

Do you see the children's ideas being implemented?

What activities would you like to see included in the program?

Discuss these with your manager.

Follow up – activity extensions.
Have you been implementing your activity extensions? If no, why not?

What could you do to change this?

If yes, reflect on this process.

"The difference between stupidity and genius is that genius has its limits." – Albert Einstein

NOTES

Plan an activity using only readily available resources. Facilitate the activity and reflect on the process.

Suggest an item for the menu: Who's idea was it? (yours/another educator/child/family)

Suggest a program activity: note whose idea it was.

Don't forget to pass these suggestions on to your manager/menu planner.

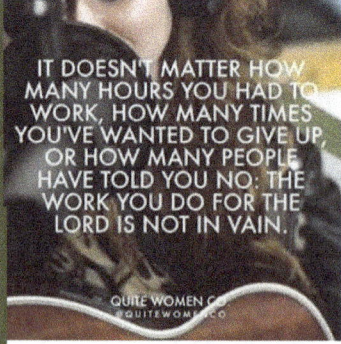

Week 4 reflection. Date: _____

Consider some professional development you would like to undertake: What would you like to learn about?

How could you achieve this?

Discuss options with your manager.

Think about an activity you did with the children….
What was the activity?

Whose idea was it?
How involved were you?

Could you have been more/less involved?
What would you change?

How can you extend on this activity? Plan to do it next week.

"If you want your children to listen, try talking softly to someone else." – Ann Landers

Follow-up: Routines
Did you discuss your routine suggestion from last week with your manager? Y/N
If No, why not?

If yes, what was the outcome?

Describe how you felt about this activity?

Consider an interaction you had with a manager this week.
Was it positive/negative? Why?

Would you have done something different? Why/why not?

Did this interaction affect your relationship with them? How?

What did you learn? How will this be reflected in your practise?

NOTES

"This then is the first duty of an educator: to stir up life but leave it free to develop."
~ Maria Montessori

Suggest an item for the menu: Who's idea was it? (yours/another educator/child/family)

Suggest a program activity: note whose idea it was.

Don't forget to pass these suggestions on to your manager/menu planner.

Follow up – interactions:
Read over your interaction reflections from the past few weeks: do you notice any patterns?

Do you focus on mainly negative or positive interactions, or a mix of both? Why do you think this is?

Week 5 reflection. Date: _____

Reflect on your physical environment.
Did you make any of the changes you wanted to see last time? Y/N. If No, why not?

If yes, reflect on how this change has impacted the service.

Dot point 1 thing you like, and 1 you would like to change now.

Compliment a co-worker on their work. Be specific and genuine. **Reflect:**
What did you say?

How did they respond?

How did you feel?

Observe over the next few days/shifts: Did this affect your relationship with this person? How?

Consider an interaction you had with a member of the school community this week.
Was it positive/negative? Why?

Would you have done something different? Why/why not?

Did this interaction affect your relationship with them? How?

What did you learn? How will this be reflected in your practise?

Think about an activity you did with the children….
What was the activity?

Whose idea was it?

How involved were you?

Could you have been more/less involved? What would you change?

How can you extend on this activity? Plan to do it next week.

What do you call a dinosaur that is sleeping?
A dino-snore!

NOTES

Reflect on staffing and the relationships between educators: Do you think these factors affect the emotional environment for children? Why or why not?

Dot point 1 thing that is working well, and 1 you would like to change. Explain why:

Suggest an item for the menu: Who's idea was it? (yours/another educator/child/family)

Suggest a program activity: note whose idea it was.

Don't forget to pass these suggestions on to your manager/menu planner

Week 6 reflection. Date: _____

What did the left eye say to the right eye?
Between us, something smells!

Consider an interaction you had with a child this week.
Was it positive/negative? Why?

Would you have done something different? Why/why not?

Did this interaction affect your relationship with them? How?

What did you learn? How will this be reflected in your practise?

Follow up – activities.
Read over your activity reflections from the last few weeks: is there a theme developing (e.g. craft/cooking/sport)?

Do you write about a variety of children or a similar group each week?

Try to focus on a different type of activity or group of children this week.

Think about an activity you did with the children….
What was the activity?

Whose idea was it?

How involved were you?

Could you have been more/less involved? What would you change?

How can you extend on this activity? Plan to do it next week.

Pick a child with whom you have mainly negative interactions. Plan positive interactions with the child. Try to double the number each day i.e. 1 on Monday, 2 on Tuesday, 4 on Wednesday etc.
Reflect: did you achieve the goal? Why/why not?

What did you learn about the child?

Did you notice any change in the child's attitude towards you? Explain:

Did you notice any change in your attitude towards the child? Explain:

How will this affect your work with this or other children?

NOTES

If you are going through hell, keep going. - Winston Churchhill

Suggest an item for the menu: Who's idea was it? (yours/another educator/child/family) Suggest a program activity: note whose idea it was. Don't forget to pass these suggestions on to your manager/menu planner	**Follow up- Menu:** Have you been sharing your menu suggestions with the person who plans menus at your service? If no, why not? Have any of your suggestions been implemented? How do you feel about this?

Week 7 reflection. Date: _____

Reflect on the services routines:
Have the routines changed in the last month? If yes, how?

Dot point 1 thing you like and 1 that you would like to change and how the change might benefit the service.
*Discuss this with your manager.

Research the Aboriginal 8 ways of learning**. Pick one element that you think your service does well. How would you explain this to a parent or ECEC assessor if they asked?

"Children today are tyrants. They contradict their parents, gobble their food, and tyrannize their teachers."- Socrates (469-399 B.C.E)

Think about an activity you did with the children….
What was the activity?

Whose idea was it?
How involved were you?

Could you have been more/less involved?
What would you change?

How can you extend on this activity? Plan to do it next week!

Consider an interaction you had with a parent this week.
Was it positive/negative? Why?

Would you have done something different? Why/why not?

Did this interaction affect your relationship with them? How?

What did you learn? How will this be reflected in your practise?

NOTES

Follow up – Program:
Discuss how your program ideas have been implemented in the program, or, if they haven't, why, and what could you do to change this?

Suggest an item for the menu: Who's idea was it? (yours/another educator/child/family)

Suggest a program activity: note whose idea it was.

Don't forget to pass these suggestions on to your manager/menu planner

"The trouble with over-structuring is that it discourages exploration."
~ Jay Giedd, Neuroscientist, University of California

Week 8 reflection. Date: _____

Ask a co-worker (not manager) for feedback on your work generally or on a specific area. Reflect:
Why did you choose this co-worker?

What did they say?

Did you feel that their response was genuine? Why?

Did you agree/disagree? Why?

How did it make you feel?

Will your practise change as a result of this feedback? If so, how?

Plan an activity with the children using only readily available resources. Implement the activity and reflect on the process.

What goes up and down but does not move?
Stairs

Think about an activity you did with the children….
What was the activity?

Whose idea was it?
How involved were you?

Could you have been more/less involved?
What would you change?

How can you extend on this activity? Plan to do it next week.

Consider an interaction you had with a co-worker this week.
Was it positive/negative? Why?

Would you have done something different? Why/why not?

Did this interaction affect your relationship with them? How?

What did you learn? How will this be reflected in your practise?

NOTES

"Play is the highest expression of human development in childhood, for it alone is the free expression of what is in a child's soul." ~ Friedrich Froebel

Suggest an item for the menu: Who's idea was it? (yours/another educator/child/family)

Suggest a program activity: note whose idea it was.

Don't forget to pass these suggestions on to your manager/menu planner

One thing I wish my manager knew about me is….

If you're feeling brave, share this with your manager.

Week 9 reflection. Date: _____

Consider an interaction you had with a Manager this week.
Was it positive/negative? Why?

Would you have done something different? Why/why not?

Did this interaction affect your relationship with them? How?

What did you learn? How will this be reflected in your practise?

Why did the student eat his homework?
Because the teacher told him it was a piece of cake!

Think about an activity you did with the children….
What was the activity?

Whose idea was it?

How involved were you?

Could you have been more/less involved? What would you change?

How can you extend on this activity? Plan to do it next week.

Follow-up: Resources challenge.
Read through your reflection from your resources challenge last week.
Which children were involved – were they the same children as the previous time?

What kind of activity did you plan? How was it different to the first time you did this challenge?

How involved were the children in planning, setting up and implementing the activity?

How much freedom did the children have in completing the activity? (i.e. free to choose, some guidance given, complete expectation to follow instructions)

What have you learned about yourself in this process?

In what way will this affect your work?

Reflect on your physical environment:
Imagine you are a prep child entering the service for the first time. What do you see?

What do you hear?

How do you feel?

What could you do to make the environment more welcoming/inviting for new children?

NOTES

NOT MY JOB	MY JOB
FIX OR SAVE PEOPLE	LOVE PEOPLE
BE LIKED	BE AUTHENTIC
DO IT ALL	TAKE THE NEXT STEP
PLEASE EVERYONE	SPEAK MY TRUTH
HOLD IT TOGETHER	BREATHE

Follow up- Physical environment: Make an effort this week to implement the changes you noted last week. Do you notice any difference in:

The children?

Other educators?

Yourself?

Suggest an item for the menu: Who's idea was it? (yours/another educator/child/family)

Suggest a program activity: note whose idea it was.

Don't forget to pass these suggestions on to your manager/menu planner

Week 10 reflection. Date: _____

Draw or describe your idea workplace: imagine money and space are unlimited.

I really love being human, but some days I really wish I could be a fairy – Greta age 4

Think about an activity you did with the children….
What was the activity?

Whose idea was it?
How involved were you?

Could you have been more/less involved?
What would you change?

How can you extend on this activity? Plan to do it next week.

Pick a child with whom you have mainly negative interactions. Plan positive interactions with the child. Try to double the number each day i.e. 1 on Monday, 2 on Tuesday, 4 on Wednesday etc.
Reflect: did you achieve the goal? Why/why not?

What did you learn about the child?

Did you notice and change in the child's attitude towards you? Explain:

Did you notice any change in your attitude towards the child? Explain:

How will this affect your work with this or other children?

Consider an interaction you had with a member of the school community this week. Was it positive/negative? Why?

Would you have done something different? Why/why not?

Did this interaction affect your relationship with them? How?

What did you learn? How will this be reflected in your practise?

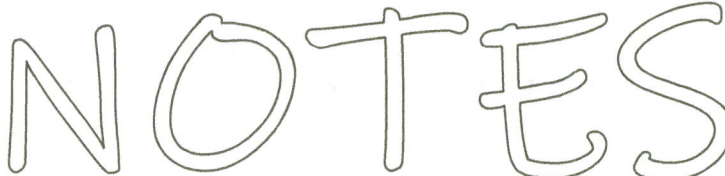

NOTES

If I had the power to change one thing at my service it would be:

Because:

Suggest an item for the menu: Who's idea was it? (yours/another educator/child/family)

Suggest a program activity: note whose idea it was.

Don't forget to pass these suggestions on to your manager/menu planner

"This then is the first duty of an educator: to stir up life but leave it free to develop."
~ Maria Montessori

Week 11 reflection. Date: _____

> What is a witch's favourite subject in school?
> Spelling!

Consider an interaction you had with a child this week. Was it positive/negative? Why?

Would you have done something different? Why/why not?

Did this interaction affect your relationship with them? How?

What did you learn? How will this be reflected in your practise?

Follow up – activity extensions.
Consider your suggested activity extension ideas. Where do your ideas come from?

Do they hold the children's interest? Explain.

Do you feel that they are extending the children's learning in the way you anticipated? Why/why not?

Consider how the routines at your service have changed in the last month.
Comment on their impact on the service (good or bad).

Suggest one way to improve the routine for afternoon tea.

Think about an activity you did with the children….
What was the activity?

Whose idea was it?

How involved were you?

Could you have been more/less involved?

What would you change?

How can you extend on this activity? Plan to do it next week.

NOTES

Suggest an item for the menu: Who's idea was it? (yours/another educator/child/family)

Suggest a program activity: note whose idea it was.

Don't forget to pass these suggestions on to your manager/menu planner

Follow-up– Strengths and challenges:

Revisit your strengths and challenges page at the beginning of this book. Have any challenges become strengths? Have any new challenges or strengths emerged? Using a different colour pen note down any changes or additions.

Week 12 reflection. Date: _____

Plan an activity with the children using only readily available resources. Try and make it completely different to your previous activities. Reflect on the process

---

Think about an activity you did with the children….
What was the activity?

Whose idea was it?
How involved were you?

Could you have been more/less involved?
What would you change?

How can you extend on this activity? Plan to do it next week.

Consider an interaction you had with a parent this week.
Was it positive/negative? Why?

Would you have done something different? Why/why not?

Did this interaction affect your relationship with them? How?

What did you learn? How will this be reflected in your practise?

What is fast, loud, and crunchy?
A rocket chip!

Set a silly goal for this week. Make it as silly as you like: What was the goal?

Did you achieve it? If no, why not?

If yes, how did you feel?

How did others react (children, parents, co-workers)?

Would you do it again? Why/why not?

NOTES

Follow up: routines.
How confident are you in discussing possible routine changes with your manager/co-workers? Explain.

Suggest an item for the menu: Who's idea was it?

Suggest a program activity: note whose idea it was.

Don't forget to pass these suggestions on to your manager/menu planner

Week 13 reflection. Date: _____

Think about the families in your service: What is the predominant family type? E.g. white, Australian, single parent.

Name one other family type that use your service and 3 ways to help them feel welcome and included.

What did the banana say to the dog?   Nothing. Bananas can't talk.

Consider an interaction you had with a co-worker this week.
Was it positive/negative? Why?

Would you have done something different? Why/why not?

Did this interaction affect your relationship with them? How?

What did you learn? How will this be reflected in your practise?

Think about an activity you did with the children….
What was the activity?

Whose idea was it?
How involved were you?

Could you have been more/less involved? What would you change?

How can you extend on this activity? Plan to do it next week.

Reflect on your physical environment.
List 3 items that the children use every day.

List 3 items that you think are essential for a service and why.

NOTES

Suggest an item for the menu: Who's idea was it? (yours/another educator/child/family)

Suggest a program activity: note whose idea it was.

Don't forget to pass these suggestions on to your manager/menu planner

Follow-up – interactions.
Read through your interaction reflections for the past several weeks: note any changes you can see in the quality of your interactions.

"You can't please everyone, and you can't make everyone like you."
-- Katie Couric

Week 14 reflection. Date: _____

> *"If you think you are too small to make a difference, try sleeping with a mosquito." – Dalai Lama*

Reflect on inclusion at your service. List 3 ways that your service helps children with additional needs to feel included.

Pick a child with whom you have mainly negative interactions. Plan positive interactions with the child. Try to double the number each day i.e. 1 on Monday, 2 on Tuesday, 4 on Wednesday etc.
Reflect: did you achieve the goal? Why/why not?

What did you learn about the child?

Did you notice and change in the child's attitude towards you? Explain:

Did you notice any change in your attitude towards the child? Explain:

How will this affect your work with this or other children?

Consider an interaction you had with a Manager this week.
Was it positive/negative? Why?

Would you have done something different? Why/why not?

Did this interaction affect your relationship with them? How?

What did you learn? How will this be reflected in your practise?

Think about an activity you did with the children….
What was the activity?

Whose idea was it?
How involved were you?

Could you have been more/less involved? What would you change?

How can you extend on this activity? Plan to do it next week.

NOTES

A Ship in Harbor Is Safe, But that Is Not What Ships Are Built For.
--John A. Shedd

Suggest an item for the menu: Who's idea was it? (yours/another educator/child/family) Suggest a program activity: note whose idea it was. Don't forget to pass these suggestions on to your manager/menu planner	**Reflect** on the services routines: describe the sign in/out routine. Note 1 strength and 1 challenge.

Week 15 reflection. Date: _____

"Laugh a lot. It burns a lot of calories." – *Jessica Simpson*

Reflect on the service program. Describe how the program is made visible and meaningful for parents.

How would you describe your program to a new parent or ECEC assessor?

Consider an interaction you had with a member of the school community this week.
Was it positive/negative? Why?

Would you have done something different? Why/why not?

Did this interaction affect your relationship with them? How?

What did you learn? How will this be reflected in your practise?

Follow up – Positive interaction challenge: revisit your first positive interaction challenge. If the child still attends your service, describe your relationship with them. Has it changed from before the challenge to now?

Think about an activity you did with the children….
What was the activity?

Whose idea was it?

How involved were you?

Could you have been more/less involved? What would you change?

How can you extend on this activity? Plan to do it next week.

NOTES

Follow up – activities: think about the way you lead activities with the children. Name one thing you do well, and one you would like help with.

Identify what you need to help you. If needed, discuss this with your manager.

Suggest an item for the menu: Who's idea was it? (yours/another educator/child/family)

Suggest a program activity: note whose idea it was.

Don't forget to pass these suggestions on to your manager/menu planner

"Success is the sum of small efforts, repeated day-in and day-out."
– Robert Collier

Week 16 reflection. Date: _____

Have you undertaken any professional development in the past 3 months? Y/N
If yes, what was it?

Was it compulsory or voluntary?

Was it offered by your company or something you self-sourced?

What professional development would you like to undertake next?

Consider the available resources at your service: name one resource and 3 unusual ways to use it. Try one with the children.

"Cleaning up with children around is like shovelling during a blizzard." – Margaret Culkin Banning

---

Think about an activity you did with the children….
What was the activity?

Whose idea was it?

How involved were you?

Could you have been more/less involved? What would you change?

How can you extend on this activity? Plan to do it next week.

Consider an interaction you had with a child this week.
Was it positive/negative? Why?

Would you have done something different? Why/why not?

Did this interaction affect your relationship with them? How?

What did you learn? How will this be reflected In your practise?

NOTES

Follow up – Menu:

Consider the menu at your service. What menu items do the children seem to enjoy most?

How many healthy choices are provided?

How would you help children make healthy choices each day?

> The best things in life are free. And it is important never to lose sight of that. So look around you. Wherever you see friendship, loyalty, laughter, & love... there is your treasure.
> — Neale Donald Walsch

Suggest an item for the menu: Who's idea was it? (yours/another educator/child/family)

Suggest a program activity: note whose idea it was.

Don't forget to pass these suggestions on to

Week 17 reflection. Date: _____

Think about an activity you did with the children....
What was the activity?

Whose idea was it?

How involved were you?

Could you have been more/less involved? What would you change?

How can you extend on this activity? Plan to do it next week

Why did the dinosaur cross the road?
Because the chicken wasn't born yet.

Consider an interaction you had with a parent this week.
Was it positive/negative? Why?

Would you have done something different? Why/why not?

Did this interaction affect your relationship with them? How?

What did you learn? How will this be reflected in your practise?

Reflect on your physical environment.
Has the physical environment changed in the past month? Y/N
If yes, in what way?

If you could set the service up any way you wanted, using only the currently available resources, how would you do it?

Compliment a co-worker on their work. Be specific and genuine. Reflect:
What did you say?

How did they respond?

How did you feel?

Observe over the next few days/shifts: Did this affect your relationship with this person? How?

NOTES

"The best teachers are those who show you where to look, but don't tell you what to see."
~ Alexandra K. Trenfor

Suggest an item for the menu: Who's idea was it? (yours/another educator/child/family) Suggest a program activity: note whose idea it was. Don't forget to pass these suggestions on to your manager/menu planner	**Follow up – program.** Look at your service's program for this week. Suggest one way to improve the program display for parents.

Week 18 reflection. Date: _____

Consider the relationship between the school and your service: would you consider it to be positive, negative, or neutral? Explain.

Do you feel there is a basis of co-operation and trust?

Do you think this affects the services program? If so, how?

Do you think this affects the children? If so, how?

List 3 ways to improve this relationship.

What do you call a dog magician?
A labracadabrador.

Think about an activity you did with the children….
What was the activity?

Whose idea was it?

How involved were you?

Could you have been more/less involved? What would you change?

How can you extend on this activity? Plan to do it next week.

Pick a child with whom you have mainly negative interactions. Plan positive interactions with the child. Try to double the number each day i.e. 1 on Monday, 2 on Tuesday, 4 on Wednesday etc.
Reflect: did you achieve the goal? Why/why not?

What did you learn about the child?

Did you notice and change in the child's attitude towards you? Explain:

Did you notice any change in your attitude towards the child? Explain:

How will this affect your work with this or other children?

Consider an interaction you had with a co-worker this week.
Was it positive/negative? Why?

Would you have done something different? Why/why not?

Did this interaction affect your relationship with them? How?

What did you learn? How will this be reflected in your practise?

NOTES

"A journey of a thousand miles begins with a single step"
--A Chinese proverb

Suggest an item for the menu: Who's idea was it? (yours/another educator/child/family) Suggest a program activity: note whose idea it was. Don't forget to pass these suggestions on to your manager/menu planner	Reflect on the service routine: name one thing you think works really well and why.

Week 19 reflection. Date: _____

Indigenous perspectives: how many indigenous children currently attend your service?

How are indigenous perspectives prioritised?

Suggest one improvement in this area.

Think about an activity you did with the children….
What was the activity?

Whose idea was it?

How involved were you?

Could you have been more/less involved? What would you change?

How can you extend on this activity? Plan to do it next week.

Consider an interaction you had with a manager this week.
Was it positive/negative? Why?

Would you have done something different? Why/why not?

Did this interaction affect your relationship with them? How?

What did you learn? How will this be reflected in your practise?

Follow -up: Co-worker interactions:
Read over your co-worker interaction reflections so far this year. Do you notice any patterns?

Do you reflect on the same co-worker or does it vary?

Do you notice any changes in yourself as a result of these reflections?

"The cure for boredom is curiosity. There is no cure for curiosity." — **Dorothy Parker**

NOTES

A sunrise reminds us that the new day is full of new opportunties

Suggest an item for the menu: Who's idea was it? (yours/another educator/child/family)

Suggest a program activity: note whose idea it was.

Don't forget to pass these suggestions on to your manager/menu planner

Look back over your physical environment reflections. Choose one that has **not** happened. What would be the benefits of that change? What challenges would it create?

Week 20 reflection. Date: _____

Choose one resource and put it out for the children to use. Without providing any guidance, reflect on what they do with it: how did they use it?

Was it what you expected?

What did you learn?

Will this affect your future programming? How?

Why are ghosts bad liars? Because you can see right through them.

Think about an activity you did with the children....
What was the activity?

Whose idea was it?
How involved were you?

Could you have been more/less involved?
What would you change?

How can you extend on this activity? Plan to do it next week.

Ask a co-worker (not manager) for feedback on your work generally or on a specific area. Reflect:
Why did you choose this co-worker?

What did they say?

Did you feel that their response was genuine? Why?

Did you agree/disagree? Why?

How did it make you feel?

Will your practise change as a result of this feedback? If so, how?

Consider an interaction you had with a member of the school community this week.
Was it positive/negative? Why?

Would you have done something different? Why/why not?

Did this interaction affect your relationship with them? How?

What did you learn? How will this be reflected in your practise?

NOTES

Suggest an item for the menu: Who's idea was it? (yours/another educator/child/family)

Suggest a program activity: note whose idea it was.

Don't forget to pass these suggestions on to your manager/menu planner

Follow up – Jokes:
Have you used any of the jokes in this book? If so, what was the reaction?

Ask the children to make up a joke and record it here.

Week 21 reflection. Date: _____

Reflect on your physical environment.
Focus on one minor change and describe the effect it has had on the service.

Intentional Teaching:
Consider a moment where you have engaged in intentional teaching over the past week or so. Which children were involved?

Was it a pre-planned or spontaneous moment?

What did you teach about?

What knowledge did the child/ren already have?

What did you learn?

Consider an interaction you had with a child this week.
Was it positive/negative? Why?

Would you have done something different? Why/why not?

Did this interaction affect your relationship with them? How?

What did you learn? How will this be reflected in your practise?

Think about an activity you did with the children….
What was the activity?

Whose idea was it?

How involved were you?

Could you have been more/less involved? What would you change?

How can you extend on this activity? Plan to do it next week.

Why do bees have sticky hair?
Because they use a honeycomb.

NOTES

Read God's Word.
Feed your faith,
and your fears will STARVE.

Suggest an item for the menu: Who's idea was it? (yours/another educator/child/family) Suggest a program activity: note whose idea it was. Don't forget to pass these suggestions on to your manager/menu planner	**Follow up – Menu:** Compare your menu to the Nutrition Australia guidelines and give it a rating: Suggest one way to improve the menu:

Week 22 reflection. Date: _____

Reflect on Cultural diversity in your service: list as many different cultures represented at your service.

Choose 1 and explain 1 way in which their expectations might differ from yours.

Why aren't dogs good dancers?
They have two left feet.

Consider an interaction you had with a parent this week.
Was it positive/negative? Why?

Would you have done something different? Why/why not?

Did this interaction affect your relationship with them? How?

What did you learn? How will this be reflected in your practise?

Pick a child with whom you have mainly negative interactions. Plan positive interactions with the child. Try to double the number each day i.e. 1 on Monday, 2 on Tuesday, 4 on Wednesday etc.
Reflect: did you achieve the goal? Why/why not?

What did you learn about the child?

Did you notice and change in the child's attitude towards you? Explain:

Did you notice any change in your attitude towards the child? Explain:

How will this affect your work with this or other children?

Think about an activity you did with the children….
What was the activity?

Whose idea was it?

How involved were you?

Could you have been more/less involved?
What would you change?

How can you extend on this activity? Plan to do it next week.

NOTES

Follow up: – One thing I wish my manager knew about me: Did you tell you manager? Why or why not?

If yes, what was the outcome?

Suggest an item for the menu: Who's idea was it? (yours/another educator/child/family)

Suggest a program activity: note whose idea it was.

Don't forget to pass these suggestions on to your manager/menu planner

"No significant learning occurs without a significant relationship."
~ James Comer

Week 23 reflection. Date: _____

Consider an interaction you had with a co-worker this week.
Was it positive/negative? Why?

Would you have done something different? Why/why not?

Did this interaction affect your relationship with them? How?

What did you learn? How will this be reflected in your practise?

Choose one element from the ideal workplace you designed in week 10: What would you need to make it happen?

Could you use resources that are already available? How?

"If you're going to tell people the truth, be funny or they'll kill you." – *Billy Wilder*

Think about an activity you did with the children....
What was the activity?

Whose idea was it?

How involved were you?

Could you have been more/less involved? What would you change?

How can you extend on this activity? Plan to do it next week.

Reflect on your physical environment and the spaces you have available to use:
How many spaces do you have?
Which spaces are used most? Why?

Which spaces are used least? Why?

Think of a different way to use one space.

NOTES

Suggest an item for the menu: Who's idea was it? (yours/another educator/child/family)

Suggest a program activity: note whose idea it was.

Don't forget to pass these suggestions on to your manager/menu planner

Reflect on your service routines: note any inconsistencies and the effect these have on the service.

Suggest one way to improve this:

Week 24 reflection. Date: _____

Set a silly goal for this week. Make it as silly as you like:
What was the goal?

Did you achieve it?
If no, why not?

If yes, how did you feel?

How did others react (children, parents, co-workers)?

Would you do it again? Why/why not?

"Life moves pretty fast. If you don't stop and look around once in a while, you could miss it." – John Hughes

Follow up – activity extensions: reflect on your activity extension ideas: do they reflect the children's needs and ideas? Explain.

Are they being implemented?
Why/why not?

Think about an activity you did with the children….
What was the activity?

Whose idea was it?

How involved were you?

Could you have been more/less involved? What would you change?

How can you extend on this activity? Plan to do it next week.

Consider an interaction you had with a manager this week.
Was it positive/negative? Why?

Would you have done something different? Why/why not?

Did this interaction affect your relationship with them? How?

What did you learn? How will this be reflected in your practise?

NOTES

> Negativity is a choice.
> Resentment is a choice.
> Anger is a choice.
> Revenge is a choice.
> Optimism is a choice.
> Compassion is a choice.
> Forgiveness is a choice.
> Empathy is a choice.
> How we live our one given life is a choice.
> *Choose wisely.*

Follow up – activity planning: consider – Where do your ideas come from?

How do you plan?

Why do you choose the plans you do?

Suggest an item for the menu: Who's idea was it? (yours/another educator/child/family)

Suggest a program activity: note whose idea it was.

Don't forget to pass these suggestions on to your manager/menu planner

Week 25 reflection. Date: _____

Consider an interaction you had with a member of the school community this week.
Was it positive/negative? Why?

Would you have done something different? Why/why not?

Did this interaction affect your relationship with them? How?

What did you learn? How will this be reflected in your practise?

Devise a resource-free activity with the children and implement it: reflect on this process.

Think about an activity you did with the children....
What was the activity?

Whose idea was it?

How involved were you?

Could you have been more/less involved? What would you change?

How can you extend on this activity? Plan to do it next week

What do you call an old snowman?
Water.

Reflect on your service program: how would you describe it to a parent or ECEC assessor? Include how you think it meets NQS guidelines.

NOTES

Reflect on professional development: have you completed any PD in the last 3 months? If not why?

Think of a PD topic you would like to explore outside of the typical childcare-related fields that might also help in your work.

Some children only survive to teenagehood because God made them cute.

Suggest an item for the menu: Who's idea was it? (yours/another educator/child/family)

Suggest a program activity: note whose idea it was.

Don't forget to pass these suggestions on to your manager/menu planner

Week 26 reflection. Date: _____

Think about an activity you did with the children....
What was the activity?

Whose idea was it?

How involved were you?

Could you have been more/less involved?
What would you change?

How can you extend on this activity? Plan to do it next week.

Follow up – Strengths and challenges:
Take a few moments to review your strengths and challenges page at the front of this book. Using a different coloured pen, make note of any changes.
Comment here about the changes you have noticed so far.

Consider an interaction you had with a child this week.
Was it positive/negative? Why?

Would you have done something different? Why/why not?

Did this interaction affect your relationship with them? How?

What did you learn? How will this be reflected in your practise?

Reflect on your physical environment:
What is your favourite area, and why?

How does this reflect in your practise?

"If you must make a noise, make it quietly." – *Oliver Hardy*

NOTES

There's always a story. It's all stories, really. The sun coming up everyday is a story. Everything's got a story in it. Change the story, change the world.
– Terry Partchett.

Suggest an item for the menu: Who's idea was it? (yours/another educator/child/family)

Suggest a program activity: note whose idea it was.

Don't forget to pass these suggestions on to your manager/menu planner

Follow up – routines:
Consider the children's toileting routines, compare this to your service's policies: do they match up? If not, how do they differ? What can be done to ensure the service is following policy correctly?

Week 27 reflection. Date: _____

Compliment a co-worker on their work. Be specific and genuine. **Reflect:**
What did you say?

How did they respond?

How did you feel?

Observe over the next few days/shifts: Did this affect your relationship with this person? How?

Consider an interaction you had with a parent this week.
Was it positive/negative? Why?

Would you have done something different? Why/why not?

Did this interaction affect your relationship with them? How?

What did you learn? How will this be reflected in your practise?

Pick a child with whom you have mainly negative interactions. Plan positive interactions with the child. Try to double the number each day i.e. 1 on Monday, 2 on Tuesday, 4 on Wednesday etc.
Reflect: did you achieve the goal? Why/why not?

What did you learn about the child?

Did you notice any change in the child's attitude towards you? Explain:

Did you notice any change in your attitude towards the child? Explain:

How will this affect your work with this or other children?

Think about an activity you did with the children….
What was the activity?

Whose idea was it?

How involved were you?

Could you have been more/less involved? What would you change?

How can you extend on this activity? Plan to do it next week

"If you could kick the person in the pants responsible for most of your trouble, you wouldn't sit for a month." – **Theodore Roosevelt**

NOTES

> A Healthy {RELATIONSHIP} doesn't drag you down. It Inspires you to be Better.

Suggest an item for the menu: Who's idea was it? (yours/another educator/child/family)

Suggest a program activity: note whose idea it was.

Don't forget to pass these suggestions on to your manager/menu planner

---

Follow up – interactions with the school community: who do you interact with most in the school community?

Explain how you make sure your interactions are professional and why you think this is important.

Week 28 reflection. Date: _____

What do you get when you cross a centipede with a parrot?
A walkie talkie.

Reflect on the emotional environment at your service: focus on the children's emotions.
What emotions do you notice the most?

What time of day do you notice them?

Does the primary mood change throughout the day/session?

How can you help support emotional resilience in the children you care for?

Reflect on your service routines: consider them from the perspective of an older child coming to the service for the first time:
Are they clear?

Do they make sense?

How do the children know what to expect?

Suggest one way to improve.

Consider an interaction you had with a co worker this week.
Was it positive/negative? Why?

Would you have done something different? Why/why not?

Did this interaction affect your relationship with them? How?

What did you learn? How will this be reflected in your practise?

Think about an activity you did with the children….
What was the activity?

Whose idea was it?

How involved were you?

Could you have been more/less involved?
What would you change?

How can you extend on this activity? Plan to do it next week.

NOTES

Follow up – emotional environment challenge: review your reflection from last week. Did you try to follow through on your suggestions to help build resilience? If yes, what was the effect?

If no, why not?

Suggest an item for the menu: Who's idea was it? (yours/another educator/child/family)

Suggest a program activity: note whose idea it was.

Don't forget to pass these suggestions on to your manager/menu planner

"In the midst of movement and chaos, keep stillness inside of you."
- Deepak Chopra

Week 29 reflection. Date: _____

Read over your reflections on the resource challenges over the past few months: what do you notice?

Set up an activity using **only** recycled or reusable materials and reflect on the children's reactions.

Consider an interaction you had with a manager this week.
Was it positive/negative? Why?

Would you have done something different? Why/why not?

Did this interaction affect your relationship with them? How?

What did you learn? How will this be reflected in your practise?

Imagine you are a child in a wheelchair. Look around your service: what do you see?

What activities are accessible?

What activities are inaccessible?

Would you feel included? Why or why not?

What could be done to create a more inclusive environment?

Think about an activity you did with the children....
What was the activity?

Whose idea was it?

How involved were you?

Could you have been more/less involved? What would you change?

How can you extend on this activity? Plan to do it next week.

Why are robots never afraid?
They have nerves of steel.

NOTES

Someone is sitting in the shade today because someone planted a tree a long time ago ~ Warren Buffett

Suggest an item for the menu: Who's idea was it? (yours/another educator/child/family) Suggest a program activity: note whose idea it was. Don't forget to pass these suggestions on to your manager/menu planner	Make a list of resources that reflect indigenous perspectives and how they are, or could be, used in the service.

Week 30 reflection. Date: _____

Think about an activity you did with the children….
What was the activity?

Whose idea was it?

How involved were you?

Could you have been more/less involved?
What would you change?

How can you extend on this activity? Plan to do it next week.

"The early bird gets the worm, but the second mouse gets the cheese." – Steven Wright

Follow up – Inclusion.
Discuss your reflection from last week with a manager or co-worker:
What was their response?

Consider an interaction you had with a member of the school community this week.
Was it positive/negative? Why?

Would you have done something different? Why/why not?

Did this interaction affect your relationship with them? How?

What did you learn? How will this be reflected in your practise?

Reflect on the physical environment at your service: where do the children eat?

Is it different at different times of the day?

What are the facilities?

How could this be improved?

NOTES

Follow up – Indigenous perspectives:
Try to incorporate indigenous perspectives and resources into every shift you work this week. Reflect on the process:

Suggest an item for the menu: Who's idea was it? (yours/another educator/child/family)

Suggest a program activity: note whose idea it was.

Don't forget to pass these suggestions on to your manager/menu planner

Once you carry your own water, you will learn the value of every drop.

Week 31 reflection. Date: _____

Consider an interaction you had with a child this week.
Was it positive/negative? Why?

Would you have done something different? Why/why not?

Did this interaction affect your relationship with them? How?

What did you learn? How will this be reflected in your practise?

"As you get older three things happen. The first is your memory goes, and I can't remember the other two." – **Norman Wisdom**

Think about an activity you did with the children....
What was the activity?

Whose idea was it?

How involved were you?

Could you have been more/less involved? What would you change?

How can you extend on this activity? Plan to do it next week.

Pick a child with whom you have mainly negative interactions. Plan positive interactions with the child. Try to double the number each day i.e. 1 on Monday, 2 on Tuesday, 4 on Wednesday etc.
Reflect: did you achieve the goal? Why/why not?

What did you learn about the child?

Did you notice any change in the child's attitude towards you? Explain:

Did you notice any change in your attitude towards the child? Explain:

How will this affect your work with this or other children?

Ask a co-worker (not manager) for feedback on your work generally or on a specific area.
Reflect: Why did you choose this co-worker?

What did they say?

Did you feel that their response was genuine? Why?

Did you agree/disagree? Why?

How did it make you feel?

Will your practise change as a result of this feedback? If so, how?

NOTES

"Every day, in a 100 small ways, our children ask, 'Do you hear me? Do you see me? Do I matter?'

Their behaviour often reflects our response."
~ L.R. Knost

Follow up – Co-worker feedback:

Read over your co-worker feedback notes. Did you ask the same co-worker each time? If so, why?

Has your practise changed as a result of any feedback you received? Why, or why not?

Suggest an item for the menu: Who's idea was it? (yours/another educator/child/family)

Suggest a program activity: note whose idea it was.

Don't forget to pass these suggestions on to your manager/menu planner

Week 32 reflection. Date: _____

Intentional Teaching:
Consider a moment where you have engaged in intentional teaching over the past week or so. Which children were involved?

Was it a pre-planned or spontaneous moment?

What did you teach about?

What knowledge did the child/ren already have?

What did you learn?

Think about an activity you did with the children....
What was the activity?

Whose idea was it?

How involved were you?

Could you have been more/less involved? What would you change?

How can you extend on this activity? Plan to do it next week.

Consider an interaction you had with a parent this week.
Was it positive/negative? Why?

Would you have done something different? Why/why not?

Did this interaction affect your relationship with them? How?

What did you learn? How will this be reflected in your practise?

What part of the fish weighs the most? The scales.

Reflect on your service routines: write down your ideal routine for a before school care session. Does it differ from the current routine? How?

What effect to you think this routine would have on the children short term?

Long term?

NOTES

Reflect on family and cultural diversity within your service.
Name the most common cultural background represented and three expectations they may have for a quality service.

Suggest an item for the menu: Who's idea was it? (yours/another educator/child/family)

Suggest a program activity: note whose idea it was.

Don't forget to pass these suggestions on to your manager/menu planner

Week 33 reflection. Date: _____

Think about an activity you did with the children....
What was the activity?

Whose idea was it?

How involved were you?

Could you have been more/less involved? What would you change?

How can you extend on this activity? Plan to do it next week.

Consider an interaction you had with a co-worker this week.
Was it positive/negative? Why?

Would you have done something different? Why/why not?

Did this interaction affect your relationship with them? How?

What did you learn? How will this be reflected in your practise?

"Of all the things I've lost I miss my mind the most." – **Ozzy Osbourne**

Follow up – intentional teaching:
Do you engage in intentional teaching each week?

What are you knowledgeable about?

What are the children interested in?

How can you use your knowledge to build on their interests?

Plan an activity with the children using only readily available resources:
What resources did you choose? Why?

What activity did you plan?

Did the activity go the way you thought it would? Why or why not?

What did you learn?

Plan an extension activity.

NOTES

Follow up – Silly goals:

Have you been trying the silly goals challenges? Why or why not?

Reflect on how this process could help you set and achieve real goals:

Suggest an item for the menu: Who's idea was it? (yours/another educator/child/family)

Suggest a program activity: note whose idea it was.

Don't forget to pass these suggestions on to your manager/menu planner

"Storms draw something out of us that calm seas don't." — Bill Hybels

Week 34 reflection. Date: _____

Consider an interaction you had with a manager this week.
Was it positive/negative? Why?

Would you have done something different? Why/why not?

Did this interaction affect your relationship with them? How?

What did you learn? How will this be reflected in your practise?

Re-read your ideal workplace design: have your ideas changed? If so how?

If you could make only one element happen at your service, which one would you choose and why?

Why did the teacher wear sunglasses to school?

Because her students were so bright.

Think about an activity you did with the children….
What was the activity?

Whose idea was it?

How involved were you?

Could you have been more/less involved? What would you change?

How can you extend on this activity? Plan to do it next week

Reflect on your physical environment: look at the way it is set up, is it generally the same every day or does it change?

Who is responsible for deciding the layout?

If the layout was vastly different, what effect do you think this would have?

If you can, try setting the environment up differently, reflect on the results.

NOTES

"A child can teach an adult three things: to be happy for no reason, to always be busy with something, and to know how to demand with all his might that which he desires."
~ Paulo Coelho

Consider an interaction you had with a member of the school community this week.
Was it positive/negative? Why?

Would you have done something different? Why/why not?

Did this interaction affect your relationship with them? How?

Suggest an item for the menu: Who's idea was it? (yours/another educator/child/family)

Suggest a program activity: note whose idea it was.

Don't forget to pass these suggestions on to your manager/menu planner

What did you learn? How will this be reflected in your practise?

Week 35 reflection. Date: _____

Set a silly goal for this week. Make it as silly as you like: What was the goal?

Did you achieve it?
If no, why not?

If yes, how did you feel?

How did others react (children, parents, coworkers)?

Would you do it again? Why/why not?

Follow up – Physical environment – outdoors.
Consider your outdoor environment: what resources are usually used in this space?

What other resources could be used?

How much time do children generally spend outdoors?

Reflect on how outdoor spaces could be used during wet weather.

Think about an activity you did with the children….
What was the activity?

Whose idea was it?

How involved were you?

Could you have been more/less involved?
What would you change?

How can you extend on this activity? Plan to do it next week.

Pick a child with whom you have mainly negative interactions. Plan positive interactions with the child. Try to double the number each day i.e. 1 on Monday, 2 on Tuesday, 4 on Wednesday etc. Reflect: did you achieve the goal? Why/why not?

What did you learn about the child?

Did you notice any change in the child's attitude towards you? Explain:

Did you notice any change in your attitude towards the child? Explain:

How will this affect your work with this or other children?

What does every birthday end with? The letter Y.

NOTES

Suggest an item for the menu: Who's idea was it? (yours/another educator/child/family)

Suggest a program activity: note whose idea it was.

Don't forget to pass these suggestions on to your manager/menu planner

"I've learned that people will forget what you said, people will forget what you did, but people will never forget how you made them feel." ~Maya Angelou

Consider the service program. List 3 activities the children participate in regularly, and one way to extend each one.

Week 36 reflection. Date: _____

Consider an interaction you had with a child this week.
Was it positive/negative? Why?

Would you have done something different? Why/why not?

Did this interaction affect your relationship with them? How?

What did you learn? How will this be reflected in your practise?

Why did the pillow cross the road?   It was picking up the chicken's feathers.

Reflect on the service routines: write your ideal routine for any After School Care session.
Is it different to the current routine? How?
If you were to implement this routine what effect would it have on the service – short term?

Long term?

Think about an activity you did with the children….
What was the activity?

Whose idea was it?

How involved were you?

Could you have been more/less involved? What would you change?

How can you extend on this activity? Plan to do it next week.

Follow up – Program.
Read over your program reflections. Have you been able to implement any changes? If so, what was the result?
If not, why not?

NOTES

Professional development.
What PD have you engaged in?

How has this improved your practise?

What PD do you plan to do next and why?

Suggest an item for the menu: Who's idea was it? (yours/another educator/child/family)

Suggest a program activity: note whose idea it was.

Don't forget to pass these suggestions on to your manager/menu planner

Leave a trail of kindness wherever you go

Week 37 reflection. Date: _____

Follow up - Activity extensions:
Reflect on your activity extensions using the prompts at the beginning of this book.

What does a cloud wear? *Thunderwear!*

Consider an interaction you had with a parent this week.
Was it positive/negative? Why?

Would you have done something different? Why/why not?

Did this interaction affect your relationship with them? How?

What did you learn? How will this be reflected in your practise?

Think about an activity you did with the children….
What was the activity?

Whose idea was it?

How involved were you?

Could you have been more/less involved?
What would you change?

How can you extend on this activity? Plan to do it next week.

Plan an activity with the children using 2 resources only. Implement the activity and reflect on the process.

NOTES

"Kids don't remember what you try to teach them. They remember what you are." ~ Jim Henson

Suggest an item for the menu: Who's idea was it? (yours/another educator/child/family)

Suggest a program activity: note whose idea it was.

Don't forget to pass these suggestions on to your manager/menu planner

Follow up – Professional development:
How many PD sessions have you attended this year?

Do you feel that they help you in your role? Why or why not?

If not, what follow up do you think is needed to make PD more beneficial for you?

Week 38 reflection. Date: _____

"Knowledge is knowing a tomato is a fruit; wisdom is not putting it in a fruit salad." – Miles Kington

Compliment a co-worker on their work. Be specific and genuine. Reflect:
What did you say?

How did they respond?

How did you feel?

Observe over the next few days/shifts: Did this affect your relationship with this person? How?

Consider an interaction you had with a co-worker this week.
Was it positive/negative? Why?

Would you have done something different? Why/why not?

Did this interaction affect your relationship with them? How?

What did you learn? How will this be reflected in your practise?

Consider your physical environment: focus on the toys and equipment in use. Imagine you are a child who has been attending the service, at least 3 times a week, all year.
Do the toys appeal to you? Why or why not?

Is there anything new?

Is there anything you really want to use? Why or why not?

Suggest one way to engage children who have seen-and-done-it-all at your service.

Think about an activity you did with the children….
What was the activity?

Whose idea was it?

How involved were you?

Could you have been more/less involved? What would you change?

How can you extend on this activity? Plan to do it next week.

NOTES

Suggest an item for the menu: Who's idea was it? (yours/another educator/ child/ family)

Suggest a program activity: note whose idea it was.

Don't forget to pass these suggestions on to your manager/menu planner

---

Re-visit your strengths and challenges page. Using a different coloured pen, record any changes.
Where have you noticed the biggest change?

"If your actions inspire others to dream more, learn more, do more, and become more, you are a leader."

-- John Quincy Adams

Week 39 reflection. Date: _____

Consider an interaction you had with a manager this week.
Was it positive/negative? Why?

Would you have done something different? Why/why not?

Did this interaction affect your relationship with them? How?

What did you learn? How will this be reflected in your practise?

Consider the environment you work in. Focus on parent behaviours. Is the atmosphere generally positive, negative, or neutral?
Why do you think this is?

Do you think parent behaviours and attitudes affect the children in care (theirs or other's)? Why or why not?

Suggest one thing you can do to encourage a positive atmosphere.

"A great pleasure in life is doing what people say you cannot do." – Walter Bagehot

Think about an activity you did with the children....
What was the activity?

Whose idea was it?

How involved were you?

Could you have been more/less involved? What would you change?

How can you extend on this activity? Plan to do it next week.

Pick a child with whom you have mainly negative interactions. Plan positive interactions with the child. Try to double the number each day i.e. 1 on Monday, 2 on Tuesday, 4 on Wednesday etc. Reflect: did you achieve the goal? Why/why not?

What did you learn about the child?

Did you notice any change in the child's attitude towards you? Explain:

Did you notice any change in your attitude towards the child? Explain:

How will this affect your work with this or other children?

NOTES

Suggest an item for the menu: Who's idea was it? (yours/another educator/child/family) Suggest a program activity: note whose idea it was. Don't forget to pass these suggestions on to your manager/menu planner	Define inclusion in your own words. How inclusive do you think your service is? Suggest one action that could make your service more inclusive.

Week 40 reflection. Date: _____

Think about an activity you did with the children….
What was the activity?

Whose idea was it?

How involved were you?

Could you have been more/less involved?
What would you change?

How can you extend on this activity? Plan to do it next week.

Reflect on your service routines. Write your ideal routine for a vacation care day. Does it differ from the current routine? How?

What would be the effect if your routine was implemented?

"I always wanted to be somebody, but now I realize I should have been more specific." – Lily Tomlin

---

Consider an interaction you had with a member of the school community this week.
Was it positive/negative? Why?

Would you have done something different? Why/why not?

Did this interaction affect your relationship with them? How?

What did you learn? How will this be reflected in your practise?

Follow up – positive interaction challenge.
Read over your interaction challenge reflections. Have you noticed a change in the way you relate to children you might term "difficult"? Explain.

NOTES

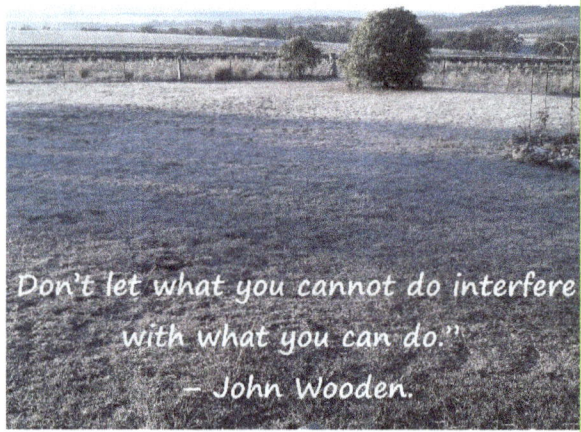

Suggest an item for the menu: Who's idea was it? (yours/another educator/child/family)

Suggest a program activity: note whose idea it was.

Don't forget to pass these suggestions on to your manager/menu planner

Follow up – Inclusion.
Read over your inclusion reflections? Write what you notice.

Do things need to change? If so, how?

Week 41 reflection. Date: _____

Think about an activity you did with the children....
What was the activity?

Whose idea was it?

How involved were you?

Could you have been more/less involved? What would you change?

How can you extend on this activity? Plan to do it next week.

Consider an interaction you had with a child this week.
Was it positive/negative? Why?

Would you have done something different? Why/why not?

Did this interaction affect your relationship with them? How?

What did you learn? How will this be reflected in your practise?

Why do you never see elephants hiding in trees?

Because they're so good at it!

Choose one resource and ask the children to plan an activity around that resource.
What resource did you choose and why?

What did they plan?

Was it what you expected? Explain.

What did you learn?

How could you extend on their idea?

Does your service acknowledge the traditional owners of the land on which you are located? If so, how?

Research your local traditional owners and suggest one way to acknowledge and honour that ownership.

NOTES

Consider your physical environment – focus on transitions.
How are transitions carried out?

Are they noticeable or do they flow throughout the day?
How do the children respond to transitions?

What could be done to make transition time easier?

"Play with reason and doubt will close all the gates"
-- Bangambiki Habyarimana, --Pearls Of Eternity--

Suggest an item for the menu: Who's idea was it? (yours/another educator/child/family)

Suggest a program activity: note whose idea it was.

Don't forget to pass these suggestions on to your manager/menu planner

Week 42 reflection. Date: _____

Consider an interaction you had with a parent this week.
Was it positive/negative? Why?

Would you have done something different? Why/why not?

Did this interaction affect your relationship with them? How?

What did you learn? How will this be reflected in your practise?

"Laughing at our mistakes can lengthen our own life. Laughing at someone else's can shorten it."– Cullen Hightower

Ask a co-worker (not manager) for feedback on your work generally or on a specific area.
Reflect:
Why did you choose this co-worker?

What did they say?

Did you feel that their response was genuine? Why?

Did you agree/disagree? Why?

How did it make you feel?

Will your practise change as a result of this feedback? If so, how?

Think about an activity you did with the children….
What was the activity?

Whose idea was it?

How involved were you?

Could you have been more/less involved? What would you change?

How can you extend on this activity? Plan to do it next week.

Follow up - Resources challenge.
What do you find most challenging about this activity?

What is easiest for you?

How can you make this more meaningful for the children?

NOTES

"Foggy road is a blessing because it is full of surprises and life is such a road! We are incredibly lucky that we all have an unknowable future!" – Mehmet Murat ildan

Follow up – Parent interactions.
Have you noticed any change in your relationships with the parents you interact with? Explain.

Do you feel that educator/parent relationships are important in the care of children? Explain.

Suggest an item for the menu: Who's idea was it? (yours/another educator/child/family)

Suggest a program activity: note whose idea it was.

Don't forget to pass these suggestions on to your manager/menu planner

Week 43 reflection. Date: _____

Think about an activity you did with the children....
What was the activity?

Whose idea was it?

How involved were you?

Could you have been more/less involved? What would you change?

How can you extend on this activity? Plan to do it next week.

Pick a child with whom you have mainly negative interactions. Plan positive interactions with the child. Try to double the number each day i.e. 1 on Monday, 2 on Tuesday, 4 on Wednesday etc.
Reflect: did you achieve the goal? Why/why not?

What did you learn about the child?

Did you notice and change in the child's attitude towards you? Explain:

Did you notice any change in your attitude towards the child? Explain:

How will this affect your work with this or other children?

Consider an interaction you had with a co-worker this week.
Was it positive/negative? Why?

Would you have done something different? Why/why not?

Did this interaction affect your relationship with them? How?

What did you learn? How will this be reflected in your practise?

Intentional Teaching:
Consider a moment where you have engaged in intentional teaching over the past week or so. Which children were involved?

Was it a pre-planned or spontaneous moment?

What did you teach about?

What knowledge did the child/ren already have?

What did you learn?

What room is impossible to enter?
A mushroom.

NOTES

Consider your routines for excursions: compare to your excursion policy. Do they match up? If not, how are they different?

What can you do to ensure policy is being followed?

Suggest an item for the menu: Who's idea was it? (yours/another educator/child/family)

Suggest a program activity: note whose idea it was.

Don't forget to pass these suggestions on to your manager/menu planner

Week 44 reflection. Date: _____

Consider an interaction you had with a manager this week.
Was it positive/negative? Why?

Would you have done something different? Why/why not?

Did this interaction affect your relationship with them? How?

What did you learn? How will this be reflected in your practise?

"Opportunity is missed by most people because it is dressed in overalls and looks like work." – *Thomas A. Edison*

Reflect on the cultural diversity at your service. Imagine you are a new child and you don't speak much English. How would you know what to expect?

Would you feel welcome and included?

What could you do to ensure all children feel welcome at the service?

Think about an activity you did with the children….
What was the activity?

Whose idea was it?

How involved were you?

Could you have been more/less involved? What would you change?

How can you extend on this activity? Plan to do it next week.

Follow up – Program:
Do you think the program displayed at your service is meaningful to parents?

Do you feel that your input is included? Explain.

Describe how the program meets NQS requirements or what could be done to meet these requirements.

How would you explain your program display to an ECEC officer?

NOTES

"Once you choose hope, anything's possible."
-- Christopher Reeve

Reflect on your physical environment – focus on the indoor space. What do you like about this space and why?

What do you dislike? How can you overcome this?

Suggest an item for the menu: Who's idea was it? (yours/another educator/child/family)

Suggest a program activity: note whose idea it was.

Don't forget to pass these suggestions on to your manager/menu planner

Week 45 reflection. Date: _____

What do you call a fly with no wings?
A walk.

Draw or describe your ideal workplace and compare it to the original one you did.
How are they the same?

How are they different?

What does this tell you about your growth as an educator?

Plan a zero-waste activity with the children and implement it. Reflect on the process.

Consider an interaction you had with a member of the school community this week.
Was it positive/negative? Why?

Would you have done something different? Why/why not?

Did this interaction affect your relationship with them? How?

What did you learn? How will this be reflected in your practise?

Think about an activity you did with the children….
What was the activity?

Whose idea was it?

How involved were you?

Could you have been more/less involved? What would you change?

How can you extend on this activity? Plan to do it next week.

NOTES

Reflect on the physical environment. Note any changes you have observed or facilitated, and the effect they have had on the service.

Suggest an item for the menu: Who's idea was it? (yours/another educator/child/family)

Suggest a program activity: note whose idea it was.

Don't forget to pass these suggestions on to your manager/menu planner

Without dreams we reach nothing. Without love, we feel nothing. And without God, We are Nothing.

Week 46 reflection. Date: _____

Consider an interaction you had with a child this week. Was it positive/negative? Why?

Would you have done something different? Why/why not?

Did this interaction affect your relationship with them? How?

What did you learn? How will this be reflected in your practise?

Observe the arrival and departure routine at your service – focussing on parent/carer drop off and pick up. What is the general routine?

How do you ensure children are only collected by authorised contacts in line with service policy?

What do you do if an unauthorised person attempts collection?

"We never really grow up; we only learn how to act in public." – Bryan White

---

Think about an activity you did with the children….
What was the activity?

Whose idea was it?

How involved were you?

Could you have been more/less involved? What would you change?

How can you extend on this activity? Plan to do it next week.

Set a silly goal for this week. Make it as silly as you like:
What was the goal?

Did you achieve it?
If no, why not?

If yes, how did you feel?

How did others react (children, parents, co-workers)?

Would you do it again? Why/why not?

NOTES

Observe the arrival and departure routines at your service, focussing on coming to and from school. What is the routine?

How do you ensure all children are present and accounted for?

Suggest an item for the menu: Who's idea was it? (yours/another educator/child/family)

Suggest a program activity: note whose idea it was.

What do you do if children arrive unexpectedly?

Don't forget to pass these suggestions on to your manager/menu planner

Week 47 reflection. Date: _____

Reflect on the program:
Who is responsible for the program planning?

Who is responsible for implementation?

Who is responsible for documentation?

If you are not directly responsible for any of these areas, note how you can have input.

"Before you judge a man, walk a mile in his shoes. After that who cares?... He's a mile away and you've got his shoes!" – *Billy Connolly*

Think about an activity you did with the children....
What was the activity?

Whose idea was it?

How involved were you?

Could you have been more/less involved? What would you change?

How can you extend on this activity? Plan to do it next week

Pick a child with whom you have mainly negative interactions. Plan positive interactions with the child. Try to double the number each day i.e. 1 on Monday, 2 on Tuesday, 4 on Wednesday etc.
Reflect: did you achieve the goal? Why/why not?

What did you learn about the child?

Did you notice and change in the child's attitude towards you? Explain:

Did you notice any change in your attitude towards the child? Explain:

How will this affect your work with this or other children?

Consider an interaction you had with a parent this week.
Was it positive/negative? Why?

Would you have done something different? Why/why not?

Did this interaction affect your relationship with them? How?

What did you learn? How will this be reflected in your practise?

NOTES

Consider your professional Development goals for this year: did you achieve them?

Was there anything you wanted to learn about but didn't? if so, why?

Set a learning goal for the next 12 months.

Suggest an item for the menu: Who's idea was it? (yours/another educator/child/family)

Suggest a program activity: note whose idea it was.

Don't forget to pass these suggestions on to your manager/menu planner

Week 48 reflection. Date: _____

Consider an interaction you had with a co-worker this week.
Was it positive/negative? Why?

Would you have done something different? Why/why not?

Did this interaction affect your relationship with them? How?

What did you learn? How will this be reflected in your practise?

Reflect on the program for Vacation Care:
Who is responsible for deciding what activities are planned?

Are all activities implemented? Explain.

Are the children's interests reflected in the program? Explain.

How do you stop a bull from charging?
You unplug it!

Review your manager interaction reflections. Reflect on them here using the reflective prompts at the front of this book.

Think about an activity you did with the children….
What was the activity?

Whose idea was it?

How involved were you?

Could you have been more/less involved? What would you change?

How can you extend on this activity? Plan to do it next week.

NOTES

Consider the quotes in this book. Do any of them resonate with you? Why?

Do you have any of your own?

Ask the children for their favourite funny quotes and record them here.

Suggest an item for the menu: Who's idea was it? (yours/another educator/child/family)

Suggest a program activity: note whose idea it was.

Don't forget to pass these suggestions on to your manager/menu planner

Surrender to what is. Let go of what was...Have faith in what will be!

Week 49 reflection. Date: _____

Think about an activity you did with the children….
What was the activity?

Whose idea was it?

How involved were you?

Could you have been more/less involved? What would you change?

How can you extend on this activity? Plan to do it next week

What word starts with the letter t, ends with the letter t, and has t in it?
A teapot!

Plan an activity with the children using only readily available resources. Try to make it completely different to the activities you usually plan. Reflect on the process.

Consider an interaction you had with a Manager this week.
Was it positive/negative? Why?

Would you have done something different? Why/why not?

Did this interaction affect your relationship with them? How?

What did you learn? How will this be reflected in your practise?

Compliment a co-worker on their work. Be specific and genuine. Choose someone you haven't complimented before. Reflect:
What did you say?

How did they respond?

How did you feel?

Observe over the next few days/shifts: Did this affect your relationship with this person? How?

NOTES

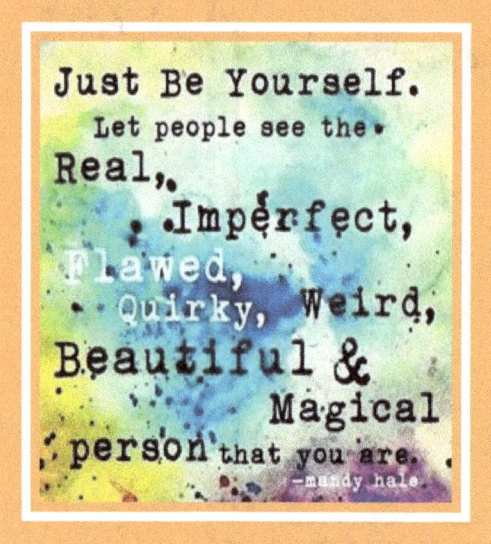

Suggest an item for the menu: Who's idea was it? (yours/another educator/child/family)

Suggest a program activity: note whose idea it was.

Don't forget to pass these suggestions on to your manager/menu planner

Reflect on your physical environment. Consider pack up time. Suggest one way to make pack up run smoothly at your service. Or, if it already does, explain the routine here.

Week 50 reflection. Date: _____

Follow up – Activity planning.
Read through your activity plans. Consider how they meet the NQS framework. Reflect on the process here.

Consider an interaction you had with a member of the school community this week.
Was it positive/negative? Why?

Would you have done something different? Why/why not?

Did this interaction affect your relationship with them? How?

What did you learn? How will this be reflected in your practise?

Reflect on environmental factors, focussing on management or upper management.
Do you feel supported? Explain.

Do you feel heard? Explain.

Do you have confidence to talk to them about any concerns you have? Explain.

If you could change one thing, what would it be, and why?

Think about an activity you did with the children….
What was the activity?

Whose idea was it?

How involved were you?

Could you have been more/less involved? What would you change?

How can you extend on this activity? Plan to do it next week.

What did the science book say to the math book?
Wow, you've got problems.

NOTES

So be *truly glad*. There is wonderful *joy ahead,* Even though you must endure many trials for a *little* while.

{1 Peter 1:6}

Follow up – Child interactions.
Reflect on your interactions with the children using the reflective prompts at the beginning of this book.

Suggest an item for the menu: Who's idea was it? (yours/another educator/child/family)

Suggest a program activity: note whose idea it was.

Don't forget to pass these suggestions on to your manager/menu planner

Week 51 reflection. Date: _____

"Worrying is like paying a debt you don't owe."
– Mark Twain

Imagine you are a child with a sensory disorder.
View your service from this perspective.
How are the noise levels?

What about light?

Movement?

What processes are in place to support children with sensory needs.

Consider an interaction you had with a child this week.
Was it positive/negative? Why?

Would you have done something different? Why/why not?

Did this interaction affect your relationship with them? How?

What did you learn? How will this be reflected in your practise?

Pick a child with whom you have mainly negative interactions. Plan positive interactions with the child. Try to double the number each day i.e. 1 on Monday, 2 on Tuesday, 4 on Wednesday etc.
Reflect: did you achieve the goal? Why/why not?

What did you learn about the child?

Did you notice and change in the child's attitude towards you? Explain:

Did you notice any change in your attitude towards the child? Explain:

How will this affect your work with this or other children?

Think about an activity you did with the children….
What was the activity?

Whose idea was it?

How involved were you?

Could you have been more/less involved? What would you change?

How can you extend on this activity? Plan to do it next week.

NOTES

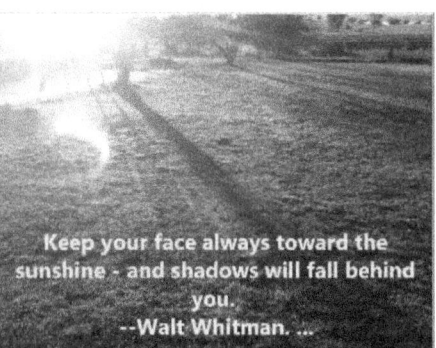

Keep your face always toward the sunshine - and shadows will fall behind you.
--Walt Whitman. ...

Suggest an item for the menu: Who's idea was it? (yours/another educator/child/family) Suggest a program activity: note whose idea it was. Don't forget to pass these suggestions on to your manager/menu planner	Read through your strengths and challenges page at the beginning of this book. Notice the changes from the first entry to the last. Celebrate your strengths. Make a plan to work on the areas you find challenging.

Week 52 reflection. Date: _____

Consider your service from the perspective of an indigenous parent enrolling their child for the first time. Is the service welcoming?

Are there indigenous resources in use or available?

Do the artworks or posters reflect indigenous perspectives?

If you needed to choose one thing to change, what would it be and why?

Think about an activity you did with the children….
What was the activity?

Whose idea was it?

How involved were you?

Could you have been more/less involved? What would you change?

How can you extend on this activity? Plan to do it next week.

Consider an interaction you had with a parent this week.
Was it positive/negative? Why?

Would you have done something different? Why/why not?

Did this interaction affect your relationship with them? How?

What did you learn? How will this be reflected in your practise?

I love all kinds of mythical creatures; unicorns, dragons, fairies, children who listen….

Reflect on this reflection process.
What was the most challenging?

What was easiest?

Was there anything you chose not to do and why?

You are welcome to provide feedback to hbrown19561@gmail.com

My Year in Review

| How has my perspective changed? | Where have I improved? |

| Have my beliefs changed? In what way? | Have my relationships changed? In what way? |

| The best thing about this year was:

Because: | The worst thing about this year was:

But I… |

CONGRATULATIONS ON A YEAR OF REFLECTION!
Don't forget to order book #2 for next year.

References and Resources:

The information in this book has been obtained from the following places. Please feel free to visit these sites for more information on any subjects in this workbook.

Jokes from: https://redtri.com/best-jokes-for-kids/slide/1

Theorist information from:

https://psmag.com/social-justice/in-memory-of-brian-sutton-smith

https://www.learning-theories.com/communities-of-practice-lave-and-wenger.html

https://en.wikipedia.org/wiki/%C3%89tienne_Wenger

https://en.wikipedia.org/wiki/Kolb%27s_experiential_learning

https://www.teachthought.com/learning/principles-of-social-learning-theory/

http://www.aral.com.au/resources/argyris.html

https://en.wikipedia.org/wiki/Kolb%27s_experiential_learning

https://en.wikipedia.org/wiki/David_A._Kolb

https://sielearning.tafensw.edu.au/MCS/CHCFC301A/12048/chcfc301a/lo/12020/index.htm#d27e389

https://en.wikipedia.org/wiki/Maria_Montessori

Information on the NQS and MTOP from:

https://www.acecqa.gov.au/sites/default/files/2018-05/my_time_our_place_framework_for_school_age_care_in_australia_0.pdf

https://www.acecqa.gov.au/nqf/national-quality-standard

https://www.acecqa.gov.au/

Recipes included in this book can be credited to Wendy Wood – who found writing them quite challenging as she rarely uses measurements when cooking.

All quotes have been credited individually where the original author is known.

Theorist reflection: Reflect on the different theorists we have looked at this year. Which ones did you agree with?

Which ones did you disagree with?

Which theory resonated with you the most? Why?

Has learning about different theorists affected the way you work with children? If so, how?

Goal reflection: Reflect on your goal for the month. Did you achieve it? If so, how? If not, why?

Personal reflection: use this space to write a personal reflection for the year.

Goal reflection: Reflect on your goals this year and the goal setting process here.

Month: _____

Reflect on Quality Area 1 – Educational program and practice Consider each area and describe your service's strengths and challenges for each area. This information can be shared with your service manager and included in the service QIP.

Standard 1.3: Assessment and planning
Educators and co-ordinators take a planned and reflective approach to implementing the program for each child.

Element 1.3.1: Assessment and planning cycle
Each child's learning and development is assessed or evaluated as part of an ongoing cycle of observation, analysing learning, documentation, planning, implementation and reflection.

Activity idea: A line-at-a-time storytelling or pictures Using a piece of paper, write one line of a story – or draw part of a picture. Leaving only the last word, or lines, showing, fold the rest of the page under and then the next person adds their input. When you reach the end of the paper open it up to see your picture or read your story.

*variation – sit in a circle and tell a story one line at a time out loud with each person taking up the story where the last left off – this works well with smaller children and those who are not confident with writing. Best done in small groups.

Goal: Set a goal for the month. Make it realistic and achievable:
What is the goal?

What steps will you take to achieve it?

How will you know that you have achieved it?

My Time Our Place – Framework for School Age Care. Reflection.
Read over your MTOP notes from the last year and reflect on the impact this has had on your work and the children you care for. Use the reflective prompts at the front of the weekly section of this book if needed.

Monthly Information and Reflection Pages

Personal reflection: use this space to write a personal reflection for the month. Use the reflective prompts at the front of the Weekly section if you need to.

Theorist Focus: Maria Montessori: 1870-1952

Maria Montessori based her method on the observation of children at liberty to act freely in an environment prepared to meet their needs. Montessori concluded that the children's spontaneous activity in this environment revealed an internal program of development, and that the appropriate role of the educator was to remove obstacles to this natural development and provide opportunities for it to proceed and flourish.

Services influenced by Montessori will have blocks of uninterrupted time for playing, exploring and using materials and equipment. Lots hands on learning opportunities within the program and the children will have the opportunity to be involved in the routine life of the service including meal preparation and cleaning.

Do you agree or disagree with this method? Why?

Do you see any influence of this theory in your service? Explain.

In what ways could this theory be applied practically in your Service?

MTOP reflection: Think about your favourite MTOP outcome – or the one that resonates with you the most. Reflect here about why you think that is, and what you can do to promote this outcome within your service.

Month: _____

Goal: Set a goal for the month. Make it realistic and achievable:

What is the goal?

What steps will you take to achieve it?

How will you know that you have achieved it?

Healthy home-made ice cream

1 cup frozen banana
1 Tbs maple syrup
1 tsp Vanilla
Additional fillings of choice (if desired)

Place all ingredients into a blender or food processor and blend until smooth. Serve immediately for soft-serve or set in freezer for 2 hours before scooping.

Additional filling suggestions.
1 cup frozen berries, mango or pineapple
2 Tbs cocoa + 1 extra Tsp maple syrup
¼ cup Mini choc-chips (add after blending)
¼ cup toasted coconut + 1Tbs coconut milk
Or anything that takes your fancy.

Reflect on Quality Area 6 – Collaborative partnerships with families and communities
Consider each area and describe your service's strengths and challenges for each area. This information can be shared with your service manager and included in the service QIP.

Standard 6.2: Collaborative partnerships
Collaborative partnerships enhance children's inclusion, learning and wellbeing.

Element 6.2.1: Transitions
Continuity of learning and transitions for each child are supported by sharing information and clarifying responsibilities.

Element 6.2.2: Access and participation
Effective partnerships support children's access, inclusion and participation in the program.

Element 6.2.3: Community engagement
The service builds relationships and engages with its community.

Goal reflection: Reflect on your goal for the month. Did you achieve it? If so, how? If not, why?

Monthly Information and Reflection Pages

Personal reflection: use this space to write a personal reflection for the month. Use the reflective prompts at the front of the Weekly section if you need to.

Goal reflection: Reflect on your goal for the month. Did you achieve it? If so, how? If not, why?

Theorist Focus: David Kolb: 1939-

Kolb's theory is an "experiential learning cycle" theory that promotes cyclic learning through 4 stages, namely: concrete learning, reflective observation, abstract conceptualization and active experimentation. **Consider each stage and write an example of how this might look in your work:**

Concrete learning, where the learner encounters a new experience or reinterprets an existing experience.

Reflective observation, where the learner reflects on the experience on a personal basis.

Abstract conceptualization, where the learner forms new ideas, or modifies existing abstract ideas, based on the reflections arising from the reflective observation stage.

Active experimentation, where the learner applies the new ideas to his surroundings to see if there are any modifications in the next appearance of the experience. This second experience becomes the concrete experience for the beginning of the next cycle, beginning at the first stage.

Where else do you see this theory in action? What does this mean for your own reflective journey?

Month: _____

Activity idea. Crazy races
Make up crazy ways to move and have races.
Try:
walking sideways
Wheelbarrow
Snail pace
Leaping
Kangaroo hop
Snake slither
Or ask the children for their suggestions

My Time Our Place – Framework for School Age Care. Focus on outcome 5: Read through the following statement from the My Time Our Place handbook. Reflect on how this is evidenced in your service and how you would describe this to an ECEC officer.

School age care settings provide unique opportunities for children to utilise their literacy and numeracy capabilities for a range of meaningful activities and life skills. Positive attitudes and competencies in literacy and numeracy are essential for children's disposition for life-long learning. In play and leisure children use their literacy and numeracy skills and understandings in practical ways. Children practice their skills and understandings and use a range of tools and media to express themselves, connect with others and extend themselves. The tools and media used are similar to those used in more formal education settings. However, through play and leisure activities children experiment and gain confidence in using strategies such as music, dance and drama and various communication technologies such as computers and DVDS to access information and to convey ideas.

Reflect on Quality Area 5 – Relationships with children Consider each area and describe your service's strengths and challenges for each area. This information can be shared with your service manager and included in the service QIP.

Standard 5.2: Relationships between children
Each child is supported to build and maintain sensitive and responsive relationships

Element 5.2.1: Collaborative learning
Children are supported to collaborate, learn from and help each other.

Element 5.2.2: Self-regulation
Each child is supported to regulate their own behaviour, respond appropriately to the behaviour of others, and communicate effectively to resolve conflicts.

Goal: Set a goal for the month. Make it realistic and achievable:
What is the goal?

What steps will you take to achieve it?

How will you know that you have achieved it?

Monthly Information and Reflection Pages

Theorist Focus: Jean Piaget: 1896-1980

Piaget proposed that the following principles underpin all cognitive development.

The child is an active learner, and, the child must be given opportunities to explore, discover and experiment. This is consistent with the MTOP framework.

He proposed 4 stages of development that all children pass through in order, however, the timeframe for passing through each stage is individual. **Consider the middle 2 stages (the ones we work with on a daily basis) and write what considerations you need to make for children in each group.**

The stages are:

Pre-operational stage – Two to seven years. In this stage children are less reliant upon senses and physical exploration and according to Piaget are 'illogical' thinkers.

Concrete operations – Seven to twelve years. In this stage which aligns with middle childhood, children are beginning to be able to demonstrate much more logical thinking. They do though need concrete materials to help them reach the correct conclusions. Thus in this stage you will see children working on mathematical problems but using blocks or counters or even their fingers to help them work out the answer.

Piaget's theory concludes that children don't think the same way as adults. This is not because children know less than adults but because their thinking processes are different. That is, school-aged children have different thinking strategies and have quite different ways of problem-solving and exploring the environment. **How does this affect our work with children? How to we adapt our strategies when we work with mixed age groups?**

Personal reflection: use this space to write a personal reflection for the month. Use the reflective prompts at the front of the Weekly section if you need to.

Goal: Set a goal for the month. Make it realistic and achievable: What is the goal?

What steps will you take to achieve it?

How will you know that you have achieved it?

Month: _____

Reflect on Quality Area 2 – Children's health and safety Consider each area and describe your service's strengths and challenges for each area. This information can be shared with your service manager and included in the service QIP.

Standard 2.2: Safety
Each child is protected.

Element 2.2.1: Supervision
At all times, reasonable precautions and adequate supervision ensure children are protected from harm and hazard

Element 2.2.2: Incident and emergency management
Plans to effectively manage incidents and emergencies are developed in consultation with relevant authorities, practised and implemented

Element 2.2.3: Child protection
Management, educators and staff are aware of their roles and responsibilities to identify and respond to every child at risk of abuse or neglect.

Goal reflection: Reflect on your goal for the month. Did you achieve it? If so, how? If not, why?

Slow cooker beef stew

1kg cubed beef
2 kg vegetables of choice – cubed
2 Tbs tomato paste
4 cups beef stock
1 tsp paprika
1 tsp cumin
1 tsp chilli
Salt and pepper to taste.

Combine all ingredients in a slow cooker. Cook on low for 6-8 hours or on high for 4-6 hours. Serve over rice or with crusty bread.
*omit beef and use vegetable stock for a vegetarian option
*beef can be swapped out for your protein of choice

My Time Our Place – Framework for School Age Care. Focus on outcome 4:
Read through the following statement from the My Time Our Place handbook. Reflect on how this is evidenced in your service and how you would describe this to an ECEC officer.
Children engage when they are motivated and can participate in purposeful activities. Further they are more likely to be confident and involved when their family and community experiences and understandings are recognised and included in the school age care setting.

Monthly Information and Reflection Pages

Theorist Focus: Argyris and Schon:

Their theory is based on the belief that people are the designers of action. That is, they design action in order to achieve their aim and monitor to see if their action was effective. They suggest that people have 2 *"theories of action"* – that which we consciously can talk about, and that which we use unconsciously.

One example they use is of a manager, when asked how he would deal with a conflict with a client, stated that he would state the conflict as he sees it and then work with the client to find a mutually agreed action. However, when recorded in this situation, he promoted his ideas and ignored those of the client.

Argyris and Schon also suggest that very few people are aware of the difference between their theories of action, and even fewer are aware of what their unconscious theories of action are.

Do you agree with this theory? Why or why not?

If you can, write an example you have observed of this theory in action, and how you can support children to recognise and develop consistent conscious and unconscious theories of action.

My Time Our Place – Framework for School Age Care. Focus on outcome 3: As educators, we have a tendency to focus on the physical element of this outcome. Read through the following statement from the My Time Our Place handbook. Reflect on how this is evidenced in your service and how you would describe this to an ECEC officer.

Wellbeing includes good physical health, feelings of happiness, satisfaction and successful social functioning. It influences the way children interact in their environments. A strong sense of wellbeing provides children with confidence and optimism which maximise their potential. It encourages the development of children's innate exploratory drive, a sense of agency and a desire to interact with responsive others. Wellbeing is correlated with resilience, providing children with the capacity to cope with day to day stress and challenges. The readiness to persevere when faced with unfamiliar and challenging situations creates the opportunity for success and achievement.

Month: _____

Reflect on Quality Area 1 – Educational program and practice Consider each area and describe your service's strengths and challenges for each area. This information can be shared with your service manager and included in the service QIP.

Standard 1.2: Practice: Educators facilitate and extend each child's learning and development.

Element 1.2.1: Intentional teaching
Educators are deliberate, purposeful, and thoughtful in their decisions and actions.

Element 1.2.2: Responsive teaching and scaffolding
Educators respond to children's ideas and play and extend children's learning through open-ended questions, interactions and feedback.

Element 1.2.3: Child directed learning
Each child's agency is promoted, enabling them to make choices and decisions that influence events and their world.

Goal reflection: Reflect on your goal for the month. Did you achieve it? If so, how? If not, why?

Activity idea.
Play rob-the-nest
Set up stations around your open play space – use buckets or hula hoops or whatever you have handy. Place one station in the centre of the others and fill it with your eggs (balls, bean bags or another small portable object) Organise the children into groups at each station, when the game starts, the children can leave their station to collect eggs from the centre – one at a time. Once the centre "nest" is empty, they can then steal from other nests until time is up. Once time is up, the team with the most eggs wins.

* judge the time for the game based on your individual group of children.

Goal: Set a goal for the month. Make it realistic and achievable:
What is the goal?

What steps will you take to achieve it?

How will you know that you have achieved it?

Personal reflection: use this space to write a personal reflection for the month. Use the reflective prompts at the front of the Weekly section if you need to.

Monthly Information and Reflection Pages

Personal reflection: use this space to write a personal reflection for the month. Use the reflective prompts at the front of the Weekly section if you need to.

Goal: Set a goal for the month. Make it realistic and achievable:
What is the goal?

What steps will you take to achieve it?

How will you know that you have achieved it?

Goal reflection: Reflect on your goal for the month. Did you achieve it? If so, how? If not, why?

My Time Our Place – Framework for School Age Care. Focus on outcome 2:

Read through the following statement from the My Time Our Place handbook. Reflect on how this is evidenced in your service and how you would describe this to an ECEC officer.

"When educators create environments in which children can contribute in meaningful ways, they are supporting children to take responsibility for their lives. Children who experience mutually enjoyable, caring and respectful relationships with people including their peers and the environment, respond accordingly. As children participate collaboratively in everyday routines, events and experiences and have opportunities to contribute to decisions, they learn to live interdependently."

Month: _____

Reflect on Quality Area 7 – Governance and leadership

Standard 7.1: Governance: Governance supports the operation of a quality service. Consider each area and describe your service's strengths and challenges for each area. This information can be shared with your service manager and included in the service QIP.

Element 7.1.1: Service philosophy and purpose
A statement of philosophy guides all aspects of the service's operations.

Element 7.1.2: Management Systems
Systems are in place to manage risk and enable the effective management and operation of a quality service.

Element 7.1.3: Roles and responsibilities
Roles and responsibilities are clearly defined, and understood, and support effective decision making and operation of the service.

Standard 7.2: Leadership: Effective leadership builds and promotes a positive organisational culture and professional learning community.

Element 7.2.1: Continuous improvement
There is an effective self-assessment and quality improvement process in place.

Element 7.2.2: Educational leadership
The educational leader is supported and leads the development and implementation of the educational program and assessment and planning cycle.

Element 7.2.3: Development of professionals
Educators, co-ordinators and staff members' performance is regularly evaluated and individual plans are in place to support learning and development.

Theorist Focus: Etienne Wenger: 1954 -
This theory focusses on Communities of Practice which can be defined, in part, as a process of social learning that occurs when people who have a common interest in a subject or area collaborate over an extended period of time Wenger defines it this way: "Communities of practice are groups of people who share a concern or a passion for something they do and learn how to do it better as they interact regularly." Note that this allows for, but does not require, intentionality. Learning can be, and often is, an incidental outcome that accompanies these social processes. **Do you agree with this theory? Why or why not?**

For Wenger, learning is central to human identity. His primary focus is learning as *social participation* – i.e. an individual as an active participant in the practices of social communities, and in the construction of his or her identity through these communities. **Reflect on how this might look in your service and how it relates to My Time Our Place outcome 1.**

Chicken Parmigiana bake.

1kg skinless chicken breast sliced or cubed
1 jar parmigiana sauce
1 cup dry breadcrumbs
1 cup grated cheese

Brown chicken in a pan then place into a baking dish Cover with parmigiana sauce, then breadcrumbs. Top with cheese.

Bake at 180° for 35-45 minutes or until cooked through.

Monthly Information and Reflection Pages

Personal reflection: use this space to write a personal reflection for the month.

Goal reflection: Reflect on your goal for the month. Did you achieve it? If so, how? If not, why?

My Time Our Place – Framework for School Age Care. Focus on **outcome 1: children have a strong sense of identity**. The list below outlines how this might look in a service. Beside each item write an example of how educators might be able to support children to:

Establish and maintain respectful, trusting relationships with other children and educators

Use effective routines to make predicted transitions

Sense and respond to a feeling of belonging

Openly express their feelings and ideas in their interactions with others

Respond to ideas and suggestions from others

Initiate interactions and conversations with trusted educators

Confidently explore and engage with social and physical environments through relationships and play

Initiate and join in play and leisure activities

Month: _____

Activity Idea:
Hold a paper plane flying competition.
Give each child 1 piece of paper to make their aeroplane. Line the children up and test their planes. Judge them on length of flight, most time in the air, most interesting flight path etc.

Reflect on Quality Area 6 – Collaborative partnerships with families and communities Consider each area and describe your service's strengths and challenges for each area. This information can be shared with your service manager and included in the service QIP.

Standard 6.1: Supportive relationships with families: Respectful relationships with families are developed and maintained and families are supported in their parenting role.

Element 6.1.1: Engagement with the service
Families are supported from enrolment to be involved in the service and contribute to service decisions.

Element 6.1.2: Parent views are respected
The expertise, culture, values, and beliefs of families are respected and families share in decision-making about their child's learning and wellbeing.

Element 6.1.3: Families are supported
Current information is available to families about the service and relevant community services and resources to support parenting and family wellbeing.

Theorist Focus: Brian Sutton-Smith: 1924-2015
In his work, *'The Ambiguity of Play'*, Sutton-Smith details seven "rhetorics" of play, or ideologies that have been used to explain, justify, and privilege certain forms of play. These seven rhetorics are progress, fate, power, community identity, imaginary, self, and frivolity. Sutton-Smith argues that the seventh rhetoric, frivolity, serves as a responsive rhetoric, in the sense that nonhegemonic forms of play are often deemed frivolous. According to Sutton-Smith, play is "a pleasure for its own sake, but its genetic gift is perhaps the sense that life, temporarily at least, is worth living." Reflect on this information and how you might use this in your service.

Goal: Set a goal for the month. Make it realistic and achievable:
What is the goal?

What steps will you take to achieve it?

How will you know that you have achieved it?

Monthly Information and Reflection Pages

Theorist Focus: Albert Bandura: 1925-

Albert Bandura, like Skinner and Watson before him, is a behaviourist. They believed that learning is gradual and continuous.

Bandura's social learning theory focuses on the imitation of behaviours by children. They will imitate their caregivers and peers, thus learning much about our society and how it operates. Through a series of experiments, he watched children as they observed adults attacking Bobo Dolls. When hit, the dolls fell over and then bounced back up again. Then children were then let loose and imitated the aggressive behaviour of the adults. However, when they observed adults acting aggressively and then being punished, Bandura noted that the children were less willing to imitate the aggressive behaviour themselves.

From his research Bandura formulated four principles of social learning. **Consider each point and how this might affect you work with children.**

1. Attention We cannot learn if we are not focused on the task. If we see something as being novel or different in some way, we are more likely to make it the focus of their attention. Social contexts help to reinforce these perceptions.

2. Retention
We learn by internalizing information in our memories. We recall that information later when we are required to respond to a situation that is similar the situation within which we first learned the information.

3. Reproduction
We reproduce previously learned information (behaviour, skills, knowledge) when required. However, practice through mental and physical rehearsal often improves our responses.

4. Motivation
We need to be motivated to do anything. Often that motivation originates from our observation of someone else being rewarded or punished for something they have done or said. This usually motivates us later to do, or avoid doing, the same thing.

Goal reflection: Reflect on your goal for the month. Did you achieve it? If so, how? If not, why?

Personal reflection: use this space to write a personal reflection for the month.

Month: _____

Reflect on Quality Area 5 – Relationships with children Consider each area and describe your service's strengths and challenges for each area. This information can be shared with your service manager and included in the service QIP.

Standard 5.1: Relationships between educators and children: Respectful and equitable relationships are maintained with each child.

Element 5.1.1: Positive educator to child interactions
Responsive and meaningful interactions build trusting relationships which engage and support each child to feel secure, confident and included.

Element 5.1.2: Dignity and rights of the child
The dignity and rights of every child are maintained.

Goal: Set a goal for the month. Make it realistic and achievable:
What is the goal?

What steps will you take to achieve it?

How will you know that you have achieved it?

Quick apple Crumble

1-2 tins apple (or fruit of choice) depending on size of baking dish
2 cups traditional rolled oats
1 cup coconut
½ cup brown sugar
1 tsp cinnamon
½ cup melted butter

Combine all ingredients except fruit and mix well
Sprinkle over fruit in baking dish
Bake at 180° until golden.

Serve with custard or low-fat ice cream

My Time Our Place – Framework for School Age Care. Focus on outcome 5: Describe how each element might look – what would you see?
Children are effective communicators

Children interact verbally and non-verbally with others for a range of purposes

Children engage with a range of texts and gain meaning from these texts

Children collaborate with others, express ideas and make meaning using a range of media and communication technologies

Monthly Information and Reflection Pages

Theorist Focus: Howard Gardner: 1943 -

Howard Gardner proposed a theory of multiple intelligences that suggests there is more than one intelligence – in fact there are 8 and possibly 9 as he is currently exploring Existentialist Intelligence. He considers children and adults to be individuals who all have skills and areas that we enjoy and excel at and that these fit into our major intelligence. For example, a child who is a capable sportsman and able to problem solve how to fit his/her body into small spaces to complete an obstacle course but struggles to complete other problem solving experiences, is more likely to fit into the Bodily-Kinaesthetic intelligence. This doesn't mean the child is unable to solve problems but is more likely to be successful when the problem or challenge relates, or the solution relates to using the body. *Give an example of this theory in practice at your service:*

Early childhood education should not be 'one-size fits all'. Not all children are academic but all children have the ability to learn, be successful and to teach others in their area of intelligence. As educators we need to provide learning opportunities for children that reflect their 'intelligence' and learning style. Knowledgeable and skilled educators should be able to assist children to transfer skills they have learn and developed into other areas. *Describe how this looks at your service:*

Gardner believed that children themselves were powerful teachers and that learning occurs in social settings. Instead of educators being the sole facilitator of learning, he saw children as 'peer mentors' assisting each other to learn and develop skills. *Is this encouraged at your service? What does it look like?*

Personal reflection: use this space to write a personal reflection for the month.

Goal reflection: Reflect on your goal for the month. Did you achieve it? If so, how? If not, why?

Month: _____

Reflect on Quality Area 4 – Staffing arrangements
Consider each area and describe your service's strengths and challenges for each area. This information can be shared with your service manager and included in the service QIP.

Standard 4.1: Staffing arrangements: Staffing arrangements enhance children's learning and development.

Element 4.1.1: Organisation of educators
The organisation of educators across the service supports children's learning and development.

Element 4.1.2: Continuity of staff
Every effort is made for children to experience continuity of educators at the service.

Standard 4.2: Professionalism: Management, educators and staff are collaborative, respectful and ethical.

Element 4.2.1: Professional collaboration
Management, educators and staff work with mutual respect and collaboratively, and challenge and learn from each other, recognising each other's strengths and skills.

Element 4.2.2: Professional standards
Professional standards guide practice, interactions and relationships.

Activity Idea.
Provide the children with sheets and pillows, tables chairs and pegs or bulldog clips and let them build cubby houses

Goal: Set a goal for the month. Make it realistic and achievable:
What is the goal?

What steps will you take to achieve it?

How will you know that you have achieved it?

My Time Our Place – Framework for School Age Care. Focus on outcome 4: Describe how each element might look – what would you see?
Children are confident and involved learners

Children develop dispositions such as curiosity, cooperation, confidence, creativity, commitment, enthusiasm, persistence, imagination and reflexivity

Children use a range of skills and processes such as problem solving, inquiry, experimentation, hypothesising, researching and investigating

Children transfer and adapt what they have learned from one context to another

Children resource their own learning through connecting with people, place, technologies and natural and processed materials

Monthly Information and Reflection Pages

Personal reflection: use this space to write a personal reflection for the month.

Goal reflection: Reflect on your goal for the month. Did you achieve it? If so, how? If not, why?

Theorist Focus: Sara Smilanski: 1922 –

Smilansky developed three stages of play. She initially based her work on Piaget's work but expanded and developed these theories. Read through the description of each and reflect on how these are seen in your service and what this tells you about the learning that is happening.

Functional play – This occurs in the first two years of life. Infants are involved in exploring objects using their body (sucking and touching) and progressing to other physical activities such as throwing.

Constructive play – This occurs when children begin to manipulate materials to create objects and patterns. They may not be representational initially but are the child's attempts at working with the materials to produce an effect.

Dramatic play – Here children are imitating the world around them through their role play. This leads to cooperative dramatic play around agreed-upon themes.

My Time Our Place – Framework for School Age Care. Focus on outcome 3: Describe how each element might look – what would you see?

Children have a strong sense of wellbeing

Children become strong in their social and emotional wellbeing

Children take increasing responsibility for their own health and physical wellbeing

Think about how you would describe this to an ECEC assessor.

Month: _____

Reflect on Quality Area 3 – Physical environment
Consider each area and describe your service's strengths and challenges for each area. This information can be shared with your service manager and included in the service QIP.

Standard 3.1: Design: The design of the facilities is appropriate for the operation of a service.

Element 3.1.1: Fit for purpose
Outdoor and indoor spaces, buildings, fixtures and fittings are suitable for their purpose, including supporting the access of every child.

Element 3.1.2: Upkeep
Premises, furniture and equipment are safe, clean and well maintained.

Standard 3.2: Use: The service environment is inclusive, promotes competence and supports exploration and play-based learning.

Element 3.2.1: Inclusive environment
Outdoor and indoor spaces are organised and adapted to support every child's participation and to engage every child in quality experiences in both built and natural environments.

Element 3.2.2: Resources support play-based learning
Resources, materials and equipment allow for multiple uses, are sufficient in number, and enable every child to engage in play-based learning.

Element 3.2.3: Environmentally responsible
The service cares for the environment and supports children to become environmentally responsible.

Goal: Set a goal for the month. Make it realistic and achievable:
What is the goal?

What steps will you take to achieve it?

How will you know that you have achieved it?

Basic Muffin Recipe (can also be used to make a slice if muffins tins are not available)

2 cups SR flour
1/3 cup oil or melted butter
¼ cup sugar (omit for savoury muffins)
1 egg
1 cup milk
1 tsp vanilla (omit for savoury muffins)
1 cup sweet or savoury filling of choice.

Combine dry ingredients in a large bowl
Combine wet ingredients and add to dry
Mix with a wooden spoon or spatula – don't over mix.
Add filling of choice and mix till just combined
Spoon into muffin pans or slice tray and cook at 200° for 12-15 minutes or until a skewer inserted in the centre comes out clean

Monthly Information and Reflection Pages

Theorist Focus: Lev Vygotsky: 1896-1934

Vygotsky's theory is called a socio-cultural theory of cognitive development. He believed that children, in different cultures, learn ways of thinking that are necessary to live in their own culture and community. He saw that social interaction and language had a major influence on the development of children's thinking. **Do you agree? Why or why not?**

Vygotsky emphasised the importance of relationships and interactions between children and more knowledgeable peers and adults. He believed that children's cognitive understandings were enriched and deepened when they were 'scaffolded' by parent, teachers, or peers (Berk 1996). **What does "scaffolding" mean to you? How do you apply this in your practise?**

Vygotsky proposed the Zone of Proximal Development – the gap between what children can learn unassisted and what children can learn when guided by an adult or a more capable peer. Educators need to have a thorough knowledge of each child. We need to be able to see when a child is becoming frustrated and would be able to gain the concept or skill if guided by the educator, thus scaffolding their learning. **Do you see this in your service? What does (or should) it look like?**

There is far too much information to include in these pages. Please research for yourself and add any information that you find interesting and useful.

Personal reflection: use this space to write a personal reflection for the month. Use the reflective prompts at the front of the Weekly section if you need to.

Goal reflection: Reflect on your goal for the month. Did you achieve it? If so, how? If not, why?

Goal: Set a goal for the month. Make it realistic and achievable:
What is the goal?

What steps will you take to achieve it?

How will you know that you have achieved it?

Month: _____

Activity suggestion.
Make playdough using your favourite recipe. Provide the children with a variety of tools – biscuit cutters, rocks, sticks, toy animals, kitchen utensils or anything else you can find. Observe what they children do with them.

My Time Our Place – Framework for School Age Care. Focus on outcome 2: Describe how each element might look – what would you see?

Children are connected with and contribute to their world

Children develop a sense of belonging to groups and communities and an understanding of the reciprocal rights and responsibilities necessary for active community participation

Children respond to diversity with respect

Children become aware of fairness

Children become socially responsible and show respect for the environment

Reflect on Quality Area 2 – Children's health and safety Consider each area and describe your service's strengths and challenges for each area. This information can be shared with your service manager and included in the service QIP.

Standard 2.1: Health: Each child's health and physical activity is supported and promoted.

Element 2.1.1 Wellbeing and comfort
Each child's wellbeing and comfort is provided for, including appropriate opportunities to meet each child's need for sleep, rest, and relaxation.

Element 2.1.2: Health Practices and procedures
Effective illness and injury management and hygiene practices are promoted and implemented.

Element 2.1.3 Healthy lifestyle
Healthy eating and physical activity are promoted and appropriate for each child.

Monthly Information and Reflection Pages

Reflect on Quality Area 1 – Educational program and practice. Consider each area and describe your service's strengths and challenges for each area. This information can be shared with your service manager and included in the service Quality Improvement Plan (QIP)

Standard 1.1: Program: The educational program enhances each child's learning and development.

Element 1.1.1: Approved learning framework
Curriculum decision making, contributes to each child's learning and development outcomes in relation to their identity, connection with community, wellbeing, confidence as learners and effectiveness as communicators.

Element 1.1.2: Child-centred
Each child's current knowledge, strengths, ideas, culture, abilities and interests are the foundation of the program.

Element 1.1.3: Program learning opportunities
All aspects of the program, including routines, are organised in ways that maximise opportunities for each child's learning.

My Time Our Place – Framework for School Age Care. Focus on outcome 1: Describe how each element might look – what would you see? Children have a strong sense of identity.

Children feel safe, secure, and supported.

Children develop their autonomy, inter-dependence, resilience and sense of agency.

Children develop knowledgeable and confident self-identities.

Children learn to interact in relation to others with care, empathy and respect

Personal reflection: use this space to write a personal reflection for the month. Use the reflective prompts at the front of the Weekly section if you need to.

Month: _____

Theorist focus: Urie Bronfenbrenner: 1917-2005

Bronfenbrenner's theory focuses of the balance between nature and nurture. The child is illustrated as being in the centre of 4 concentric circles. Read through the following descriptions and write how you think these might look.

Microsystem – in this system are the child's immediate family and surroundings:

Mesosystem – the broader surroundings and influences on the child's development. This system includes the preschool, doctor's surgery and other influences on the child's and family's life:

Exosystem – a broader circle of people who indirectly influence the child. Things in the exosystem include the parent's workplace, the services available to the family and the support networks they are involved in:

Macrosystem – this is an even broader system that includes the values, customs and attitudes of the cultural group the child belongs to:

Brofenbrenner recently modified his theory and acknowledged that the child's biological hereditary make-up combines with environmental forces to mould development.

Describe how this theory is, or could be, reflected in your work:

Pancake Recipe

2 cups SR flour
1 egg
1tsp Vanilla essence
¼ cup sugar
Enough milk to make a thin batter

Combine flour and sugar in a large bowl. Make a well in the centre.
Pour wet ingredients into the well and whisk from the inside out, adding more milk as needed.
Allow to sit for at least 10 minutes, then cook ¼ cup at a time in a hot pan, turning once set.
Serve with your favourite toppings.
*for dairy free, use water or milk alternative.

Goal reflection: Reflect on your goal for the month. Did you achieve it? If so, how? If not, why?

Goal: Set a goal for the month. Make it realistic and achievable:
What is the goal?

What steps will you take to achieve it?

How will you know that you have achieved it?

Monthly Information and Reflection Pages

Monthly Notes and Review

Welcome to the monthly section of this book!

These pages are designed to be used in order, and concurrently with the weekly pages. On these pages we have included information about the National Quality System (NQS) and the national curriculum for School Age Care, My Time Our Place (MTOP), as well as various theorists whose work has influenced Early Childhood Education and Care over the years. You will also find activity suggestions and recipes that you can use (if you want to).

We have included 2 pages per month, with information and reflective questions. Feel free to complete them at any time during the month, although I suggest having a good read through at the beginning of the month and leaving the reflective boxes till the end.

Instructions

Theorist information: Obviously we could write a whole book with this information and therefore, the information included in this book is limited. Please do your own research – there is a reference page included at the back of this section, but a google search will turn up more results than you can poke a stick at. We have included some questions to help you think about the theorists and how their theories might apply to your work with children.

NQS Focus: These boxes contain some of the information from this document. Each service must have a Quality Improvement Plan (QIP) that outlines their strengths and areas to work on in regard to the 7 Quality areas. Your reflections in these pages should be shared with your managers and can be included in your service QIP.

MTOP: We have included some information from this document, and questions, for you to reflect on. Think about your work and also how you would explain this to an Office of Early Childhood Education and Care (ECEC) assessor if they asked. MTOP is the document that ties in to the NQS quality area 1: Program and Practice; and should guide all our program and planning. There is considerably more information on this available than is able to be included here. Your service should have a copy of the booklet that you can refer to, or you can find the information on the ACECQA website. https://www.acecqa.gov.au

Goal Setting: This is an important part of our work. There is a space provided each month for you to write your goals, what steps you need to take to achieve them, and how you will know that you have achieve them. This should be completed at the beginning of each month – there is a separate reflection space to complete at the end of the month.

Personal reflection: Use this space to record your personal reflection. Be honest, don't be afraid to write how you feel – this is ultimately your reflection. While there are items throughout this book that should be shared with your managers and co-workers, this section is ultimately about you, and you don't have to share this with anyone unless you feel comfortable doing so.

So... We hope you find this book useful and informative. Feel free to provide feedback to hbrown19561@gmail.com

Happy Reflecting

www.ingramcontent.com/pod-product-compliance
Lightning Source LLC
Chambersburg PA
CBHW080855010526
44107CB00057B/2587